Aligning Resources for Student Outcomes

School-Based Steps to Success

M. James Kedro

ScarecrowEducation
Lanham, Maryland • Toronto • Oxford
2004

Published in the United States of America
by ScarecrowEducation
An imprint of The Rowman & Littlefield Publishing Group, Inc.
4501 Forbes Boulevard, Suite 200, Lanham, Maryland 20706
www.scarecroweducation.com

PO Box 317
Oxford
OX2 9RU, UK

British Library Cataloguing in Publication Information Available

Library of Congress Cataloging-in-Publication Data
Kedro, M. James (Milan James), 1946–
  Aligning resources for student outcomes : school-based steps to success /
M. James Kedro.
      p. cm.
Includes bibliographical references and index.
  ISBN 1-57886-127-6 (pbk. : alk. paper)
  1. School-based management—United States. 2. Academic
achievement—United States. I. Title.
LB2806.35.K43 2004
371.2—dc22   2004000078

∞™ The paper used in this publication meets the minimum requirements of
American National Standard for Information Sciences—Permanence of
Paper for Printed Library Materials, ANSI/NISO Z39.48-1992.
Manufactured in the United States of America.

Physical Processing

Order Type: NTAS

Sel ID:
6799

Cust/Add: 228470005/01   JFGC   FLORIDA GULF COAST UNIVERSITY

Cust PO No.   P0006214   **Cust Ord Date:**   9/30/2004

BBS Order No: C124940   Ln:89   Del:1   **BBS Ord Date:**   10/1/2004 1:54:43

1578861276-18270565   **Sales Qty:** 1   **#Vols:** 001

Aligning resources for student outcomes

Subtitle:school-based steps to success   Stmt of Resp:M. James Kedro.

PAPERBACK   **Pub Year:**2004   **Vol No.:**   Edition:

Kedro, M. James .

Scarecrow Education   **Ser. Title:**

Tech Services Charges:
PromptCat Barcode US   Base Charge Processing   Property Stamp US
Kapco US   Spine Label PromptCat   Security Device US
Barcode Label   Spine Label Protector US   TechPro Cataloging US
Barcode Label Protector   CD ROM US

Cust Fund Code: EDU05-1000   **Cust Location:**
Stock Category: **Cust Dept:**FGAA

Order Line Notes

Notes to Vendor   ;

540604

To all who are the St. Louis public schools

Good education will be fully effective only when there are good social conditions and, among individuals, good beliefs and feelings; but social conditions, and the beliefs and feelings of individuals will not be altogether satisfactory until there is good education. The problem of reform is the problem of breaking out of a vicious circle and of building up a virtuous one in its place.

—Aldous Huxley, *Ends and Means*, 1937

Contents

Preface

The pendulum of education swings, it seems, locked in clock works that afford little room for freedom of movement. Back and forth we go into a future already upon us. For the last century, the methodologies of public education have swung to and fro from centralized, tight-knit, top-down control of the instructional domain to progressive, open-minded, school-directed management of what's supposedly best for student academic performance.

When the schoolhouse clock runs smoothly, when resources abound for all manner of educational innovations—proven or not, staff members adequately trained or not—the restraints on school-level leadership somehow lessen. But when the clock spring of school finance becomes wound too tightly, when our resources contract and our supports shrink, public education frequently snaps back toward more traditional, sometimes outmoded practices.

This book does not purport to contain a solution to the above quandary. No one has all the answers to the multiple dilemmas that confront public education and, in turn, affect improvements in student academic performance. However, the chapters in this text offer practical suggestions for school leaders to consider as they search for direction, obtain their bearings, and establish a course of action to help school staff members and students achieve successes.

If nothing else, two decades affiliated with a large public school system has impressed upon me several important requisites for cultivating excellence in academic performance. Genuine improvement is found in well-trained leaders, collegial teamwork, and coherent programs designed, maintained, and fine-tuned at the school level. Nonetheless, the questions I've posed and the ideas I've assembled here will not satisfy the needs of all who are concerned with aligning resources to raise the levels of student achievement in their schools.

This work is but one pathway toward uplifting academic perform-ance. It is written for those school staff members who wish to travel the road of self-directed, personal accountability, those who have made the decision to take control of school leadership, management, and fiscal practices. These practices, I believe, should stand firm in the winds of central-office change and not vacillate or collapse under the strain of economic cycles.

The school-based practices discussed here, if implemented wisely, should produce academic results. Ultimately, however, your school leadership team must regularly establish its own best practices and de-sign its own road map to success, always with modifications along the route to suit the ever-changing needs of your school. This can only hap-pen when school administrators, teachers, and students establish frank and open communication about "the good, the bad, and the ugly" in the school.

Effective school leaders already know that a wide array of school-based practices are available that will upgrade academic achievement. The correct menu of resources must be selected and appropriately ap-plied, and this must be accomplished within the fiscal limitations found in your school.

Today's schools must lift all students to higher levels of performance and do so with diminishing resources. Thus, aligning school resources for success must follow many directions and occur on many levels and dimensions. What works in one school may or may not serve the needs of another. This should be no revelation to instructional staff members who have replicated what appear to be worthwhile educational reforms only to meet with little success.

One thing I've learned from evaluating standards, leadership, in-struction, and programs is that every school must necessarily develop its own leadership style. Administrators and teachers need to learn from each other as a committed, motivated group that bands together to accomplish the school mission. Each school needs a leadership team that together can find the answers that will sustain high levels of academic performance in response to the school's unique educational circumstances.

Many educators have long proclaimed that it's time to break the time-worn mold of education that proved so useful in the industrial age. We've come to see that the old-style regimentation of teaching and learning strangles innovation and restrains efficient decision making in today's public schools. As Alvin Toffler put it more than 20 years ago in *The Third Wave* (1980), society will come to recognize the value in decentralized decision making. "Such changes imply a striking shift away from standard old-fashioned bureaucracy," wrote Toffler, "and the emergence in business, government, the schools, and other institutions of a wide variety of new-style organizations" (p. 337).

More than two centuries ago, one of our nation's founders expressed an educational aphorism that continues to be pertinent for each generation. John Adams wrote that for great things to be accomplished, "a memorable change must be made in the system of education and knowledge must become so general as to raise the lower ranks of society nearer to the higher" (McCullough, 2001, p. 364). The recognition of wide disparities in the educational attainments within our society is not new. Each generation of Americans has had to face the challenge of "closing the achievement gap."

As a step toward the elimination of the achievement gap, I contend that the pendulum in the schoolhouse clock needs to be replaced with educational systems that fit the rapidly changing, technologically oriented, culturally diverse information age in which we live. Families and children who seek the opportunities that await them in this new age have hoped too long for improvements in public education. They should expect no less than a complete and relevant revamping of our schools so that youth may obtain the knowledge and demonstrate the essential skills the world will require.

However we approach solutions to improve education, by now all should know that a public school is a social and economic microcosm of the community it serves. A school is our investment in the future, an extended family imparting knowledge to each new generation. It can be dysfunctional or it can be nurturing. Most likely, a school is an admixture of positive and negative influences searching for a workable equilibrium. To find proper balance and meet the needs of a changing society, school leaders must learn to adopt and adapt. What may have satisfied the requirements of one generation may not necessarily fit the needs of another.

The people touched by the school, all those who comprise it—students, parents, teachers, administrators, and members of the community—must collectively grasp the reins of school leadership. More than two decades ago in *Free to Choose* (1979), Milton and Rose Friedman asserted: "One way to achieve a major improvement, to bring learning back into the classroom, especially for the most disadvantaged, is to give all parents greater control over their children's schooling" (p. 160).

While I may not subscribe to every educational theory advocated by the Friedmans, I wholeheartedly concur that parents generally have more interest in their children's schooling and needs than anyone else. Parents and the larger community must be part of the equation that will provide the solution to improve academic outcomes for all children.

When the people who are the school take the initiative and apply their strengths to create faculty and student successes, good things begin to happen. Certainly, as attested to by the resources cited in this book, plenty of help is available. But no one on the outside looking in—well-meaning educational bureaucrats, political entities, media gurus, corporate directors, management restructuring teams, or community leaders—can make an effective school. It's up to those who are the school to remain vigilant, to regularly restructure and align resources toward the school's primary mission, improved academic performance.

Acknowledgments

My acknowledgments may be a bit longer than what's typical because this book could not have been written without considerable input from others. Throughout the text, I have relied upon the writings and Internet postings of many educators and researchers. I trust my indebtedness to their work is evident in my list of references, the ideas of those who supplied direction to this study.

Having labored in publishing for many years, including work as a managing editor for the North Central Association of Colleges and Schools, I value the contributions an editor brings to the development of a manuscript. Several editors deserve mention for their assistance in seeing this work through to completion.

First, I thank Jan Umphrey, editor of *Principal Leadership*, published by the National Association of Secondary School Principals. Jan requested that I write an article on the topic of school finance and school-based management. That article ultimately led to this book. Portions of several chapters here first appeared in *Principal Leadership*. With associate editor Michelle McKinley, Jan Umphrey improved upon the readability of my work. I'm grateful to the National Association of Secondary School Principals for permission to use my articles here.

Material in the text that covers aspects of teacher professional development is awaiting publication in the *Journal of Staff Development*, ably edited by Valerie von Frank. An article on evaluating teacher training that I coauthored with colleague William E. Short will be forthcoming in that journal. I thank the National Staff Development Council, publishers of the *Journal of Staff Development*, for allowing me to use portions of that manuscript here.

Among editorial contributors deserving special note is Dr. Thomas F. Koerner, vice president and editorial director of ScarecrowEducation. This book would not have been possible, nor would it have been envisioned or begun, without his patient counsel. Thanks also are due to Cindy Tursman, managing editor of ScarecrowEducation, whose talents turned a raw manuscript into a usable resource.

From the mid-1980s, I have tried in my small way to contribute to the improvement of education in the largest school system in Missouri, the St. Louis public schools. Central-office administrators, school principals and site-level leaders, program directors, classroom teachers, and students and families have shared their knowledge in helping me to evaluate the implementation of instructional programs and academic outcomes. The collective commitment and perseverance of these concerned people in the face of incredible challenges often go without recognition or reward. Therefore, I thank all who gave freely of their time whenever I approached them for assistance.

I am especially indebted to my colleagues in the Division of Research, Assessment, and Evaluation in the St. Louis public schools. Their unremitting attention to accuracy and objectivity provides the schools with the means for data-driven leadership. For two decades it has been my privilege to work with them. Much information in this book depended upon the skills of fellow evaluators in data collection, analysis, interpretation, and the timely dissemination of useful information.

I also wish to acknowledge the faculty and staff on the Meramec campus of St. Louis Community College. My affiliation with the college gives me a firsthand opportunity to keep in touch with the classroom. For almost two decades as an adjunct faculty member in the Department of History, I've kept abreast of new instructional methodologies, learning strategies, and educational issues affecting a diverse student population.

I cannot recall a time when I have not been surrounded by issues that involve the education of children and young adults. My mother, a music instructor and teacher for 30 years, nurtured her family with an appreciation for learning and knowledge. I still encounter people in the St. Louis metropolitan area who, upon hearing my name, ask if I am related to their kindergarten teacher, Mrs. Kedro (now retired for almost 20 years). Such is the impact and influence of the effective teacher on the young mind—and the family.

One of my sisters is renowned as an educator in family and consumer science in Wyoming. A younger sister is a preschool teacher and educator in the highly successful Missouri Parents as Teachers Program. Each in their way, without realizing it, contributed to this book.

Another Mrs. Kedro, my wife Prudence, is a teacher and the librarian in a middle school. Her skill in maneuvering me through computer programs never fails to amaze me. She has assisted in the completion of many tasks, including those required for this project.

Having helped to raise four children, each of whom received academic honors in public and private schools, lends some credence, I hope, to my thoughts on education. Each of my children successfully graduated from college, and from faraway homes they continue to offer their personalized input on teaching and learning. My son bolsters his university degree in economics with training designed to meet the needs of a national rail carrier. My oldest daughter teaches mathematics; my youngest is applying her degree in fine arts and film studies toward pursuits in Montessori education. I am indebted to yet another daughter, Laura Kedro, artist, animator, and graphic designer, for her editorial expertise in the preparation of this text and its index.

My interests have always embraced popular culture, and I often infuse into my instruction contemporary social, political, or economic concerns drawn from today's electronic media. On occasion, I use movies as fictional case studies reflecting larger historical concepts or relevant behavioral issues analogous to the topics I'm examining. Therefore, I offer a hardy thanks to Hollywood, for I've utilized several films in this volume. Perhaps you know of these movies. Or perhaps when the opportunity presents itself to view one on late-night TV or a cable channel, you'll connect again to an idea that you'll have encountered among these chapters.

This book was written as a primer to explore school-based practices for the acquisition of all manner of resources, tangible and intangible. As educators, we share a common goal, to uplift instruction and learning in our schools. I have borrowed liberally from the thoughts of many educators and profited from their theories. As you search these pages for ideas, however, any misinterpretations or shortcomings in presentation, perceived or actual, are my responsibility alone.

Following the Research Road

In the classic film *The Wizard of Oz* (1939), Dorothy must follow the yellow brick road to the Emerald City and learn for herself how to get home. "But how do I start for the Emerald City?" she wants to know. "It's always best to start at the beginning," she's told. Sound advice. And a beginning usually requires a look into the past. For our purposes, this includes a brief review of selected literature and a glimpse into school districts that have made use of school-based or site-based management (SBM).

More than one-third of the nation's school districts have implemented some form of SBM. The number is growing, and variations on the SBM theme flourish. Generally, SBM refers to the decentralization of school administration, a shift away from central-office bureaucracy toward greater oversight at the school level. Roles are restructured so that the school system's administrators assist and support frontline workers—principals, teachers, parents, and students. The school, in exchange for expanded control of its operations, assumes greater accountability for its achievement results.

Whatever the formats of SBM, at center stage are the watchwords *staff empowerment* and *shared decision making*. Other important elements include managerial knowledge, access to information, and rewards for performance.

When we look for a star in the SBM script, research consistently identifies on-site budgetary control. How school-based budgeting is cast, however, differs widely among districts and sometimes among the schools within a district. And like other programs, proficiency in using SBM to search out resources depends upon active principal participation. The principal must work in league with key leadership players who represent the school's teachers, parents, and community supporters. An ongoing analysis of school finances is essential because SBM is a living process, ever adjusting to the changing needs of the school and its community.

Districts adopt SBM for a variety of reasons. The impetus to move to SBM may result from shortfalls in state and local government appropriations to the schools or demands for greater accountability at the school level, or both. Regardless, the goal should always be improved student achievement, which in some schools requires closing an achievement gap based on socioeconomic factors in the student population.

How do schools acquire worthwhile resources that aid in uplifting student achievement? As you seek answers, you'll encounter setbacks and pitfalls along the SBM trail. Like Dorothy and her friends in the enchanted forest, you may even see the signpost "I'd Turn Back If I Were You." Keep in mind that SBM holds the promise of improved academic achievement, but unfortunately, like other educational programs, it's not the ruby slippers.

Studies that focus on SBM for budgetary control and fiscal management are extensive. This book cannot visit all of them. Traversing the research road that leads to successful resource acquisitions need not be an arduous journey. Much helpful information is available, and it's usually easily accessible. But along the way we must be wary of witches and wizards. It's up to each school staff member to stay focused on getting home, that is, on doing the groundwork that will result in resource acquisitions to help accomplish the school mission of improved academic outcomes.

In flush times and in periods of economic belt-tightening, school-based fiscal practices can be an important tool in getting the most out of allocations and in gathering needed support. The techniques discussed in the chapters that follow may help, too, in aligning school-level operations to promote the best utilization of available resources.

STUDIES BY CENTERS, ORGANIZATIONS, AND UNIVERSITIES

School staff members who wish to develop a comprehensive understanding of SBM strategies should start by investigating the evolution of SBM and its facilitative component, school-based budgeting. As demands for greater productivity and accountability continue to be placed upon public school systems, reform strategies that involve increased school-site authority over the budget have grown in popularity. When properly implemented, site-based budgeting has the potential to promote staff collegiality, foster instructional innovations, expand financial equity among schools, and improve student achievement.

Site-based management is as diverse as the states and school districts that implement it. SBM can be initiated informally at the school level, by a board-authorized districtwide mandate, or by state law. For example, while Texas and Maryland require school-based councils, those councils do not wield the authority over budgetary matters and school policy that the councils in Kentucky are granted. And when they adopted SBM in their states, Illinois and Colorado legislators focused on their biggest urban districts, Chicago and Denver. Requirements for those who may hold school council membership vary among districts also.

To keep abreast of SBM happenings, a variety of education consortiums, associations, organizations, and government agencies conduct studies of site-based decision making and fiscal oversight. University think tanks have produced significant white papers on the topic. The Office of Educational Research and Improvement (OERI) in the U.S. Department of Education funds and disseminates investigations (some cited throughout this book) that explain and assess SBM practices. Financial support for these studies also comes from foundations such as the Carnegie Corporation of New York. Together, the reports done by these groups afford a wealth of information. Many publications and Internet sites can be used to assist local school administrators and teachers in planning for and developing workable on-site budgets geared toward improved academic outcomes.

Education Research Centers

A helpful place to start your investigation of SBM is the Internet. An Educational Resources Information Center (ERIC) search could lay the foundation on which to build a site-specific plan. The amount of time or the staff support that you have available for research will dictate the depth and breadth of your examination. Be warned, the stack of SBM studies by academicians and practitioners that piles up on your desk could rival a skyscraper. Selectivity in sources, a focus on down-to-earth issues, and a healthful dose of skepticism should remain your bywords. With that in mind, useful allies in research endeavors are the educational resource centers strategically located around the nation to serve geographic regions. Each center provides considerable information on site-based budgeting as well as links to worthwhile Internet sites.

For instance, the New England Comprehensive Assistance Center (NECAC) currently devotes a portion of its Internet site specifically to "Site Based Management." NECAC links to a variety of on-line materials that answer questions about SBM and direct you to helpful resources. On the other side of the nation, the Northwest Regional Education Laboratory (NWREL), like most regional centers, allows you to enter a search term on its home page, then identifies and provides multiple links treating all aspects of your inquiry, including SBM.

Don't be discouraged if the link to an important Web page listed by an educational resource center no longer connects and opens. Often you can use the link's name as a lead, enter it on a search engine like Google, and find that the source you're looking for is still on the World Wide Web but under a new URL. (Several educational resource centers and their URLs appear in the references cited throughout this book.)

National School Collaboratives

Along with educational resource centers, important sources of information and assistance are school-district collaboratives and consortiums. For example, the Cross City Campaign for Urban School Reform (CCC), headquartered in Chicago, welcomes you to its Internet site with the pointed comment: "If you want to know what your school system's priorities are, follow the money" (2000a). Certainly, the school budget is the road map to the location of a district's top-drawer preferences. CCC's site-based budgeting and school-based management program currently assist local educators in nine urban systems. Their aim is to unravel the mysteries of financial decision making. Districts served include Baltimore, MD; Chicago, IL; Denver, CO; Houston, TX; Los Angeles, CA; New York, NY; Oakland, CA; Philadelphia, PA; and Seattle, WA.

While school-based management alone will not improve achievement outcomes, the CCC says that school-site control over spending is a "powerful tool" to accomplish academic goals. The CCC program views

SBM as a three-pronged process: (1) principals, teachers, and parents work together to plan and manage school resources for improved student outcomes; (2) central-office directors decentralize decision-making and budget management responsibilities; and (3) detailed training is provided in school budgetary processes.

Another education collective, the Council of the Great City Schools (CGCS), is headquartered in Washington, D.C. Its education finance task force produces reports shared among school systems nationwide. A coalition of more than 50 of the nation's biggest urban school systems, the CGCS mission is "to advocate for and to assist in the improvement of public education in the nation's major cities" (2002a). Analyses by the CGCS of state funding and achievement levels in the public schools of Baltimore, New York, and Philadelphia afford beneficial examinations of school systems that use elements of school-based management and fiscal oversight.

A useful look into schools that accomplished academic reform was done by the CGCS (2002b) in association with the Manpower Demonstration Research Corporation (MDRC). *Foundations for Success* presents case studies of four school systems. The four districts were chosen because, among several criteria, they showed improvements in student achievement while narrowing the gap between white and minority test scores (think "No Child Left Behind"). The districts examined include the Houston (TX) Independent School District, the Charlotte-Mecklenburg (NC) Schools, the Sacramento City (CA) Unified School District, and a portion of the Chancellor District in New York City (NY).

Interestingly, the school systems in *Foundations for Success* shared several recognizable challenges (e.g., low standardized test outcomes, high teacher turnover, unchallenging curriculum, high student mobility). In each of the districts, educators had to confront and surmount these and other barriers on the road to success. A critical issue in each district was the lack of systemwide instructional coherence. This was due in part, the study determined, to weak alignment between school instruction and state standards. Ironically, the splintering of district initiatives and curricula was also attributed to *experimentation* with site-based management. Experimentation is italicized here because it is an important distinction, quite different from effective implementation. In these cases, SBM contributed to multiple, perhaps conflicting, strategies, which confounded the educational objectives sought. Due to this state of affairs, researchers reported:

> This often proved confusing to school-level staff and difficult for the district to support. Additionally, the professional development strategy was fragmented; professional development was not focused on a consistent educational strategy (either of instruction or curricula) and often consisted of one-shot workshops on a series of topics. (CGCS, 2002b)

To achieve their trend of academic success, the districts in the CGCS study stopped letting individual schools devise their own strategies (thus, eliminating one element of SBM). Rather, the districts implemented systemwide curricula and educational practices, advancing districtwide instructional coherence as a top priority. This should give the reader pause to consider that all facets of SBM may not work in all situations. Poor planning, weak implementation, or misalignment of SBM policies with state standards, district goals, or school needs will likely result in circumstances similar to those outlined above.

As with any program, its overall fit into the system and the joint effort expended to put it into action are critical to its effectiveness. SBM cannot be implemented as a shot-in-the-dark, quick fix. It's a program that demands a long-term commitment in order to realize results.

University Studies

Clarity in a school site's budgeting processes and goals is a prerequisite to academic success. This is borne out time and again in examinations of selected schools in SBM districts, schools that see positive achievement results using site-based budgeting.

For example, the Finance Center of the Consortium for Policy Research in Education (CPRE) in the University of Southern California (USC) has produced a string of school-site studies focused on SBM. The CPRE was joined in its SBM project by the Center for Effective Organizations in the USC School of Business. Their investigation took an international approach.

One report by the CPRE points to the complexities that abound in school-based budgetary systems. Twenty-seven school sites within five districts were chosen for study. The selected schools achieved varying degrees of effectiveness in their use of site-based fiscal management.

The first districts in the study included Jefferson County, KY; Prince William County, VA; San Diego, CA; Edmonton, Alberta (Canada); and Victoria, Australia. Later, the CPRE's SBM project added studies of schools in Bellevue, WA; Chicago, IL; Denver, CO; and Milwaukee, WI (Wohlstetter & Van Kirk, 1995).

In the above research, Wohlstetter and Mohrman (1994) identified factors that contribute to the success of school-based budgeting. Most revealing, teachers in the SBM schools were viewed as "entrepreneurial." They were self-directed in searching for and learning about new educational ideas. Teacher "work teams" actively pursued ideas to promote results-oriented instructional change.

Just as importantly, the schools in the CPRE study that achieved success did not wait around for the central office to come up with extra resources. School staff members independently uncovered and made available the time and the materials required to accomplish their instructional objectives. These schools proactively garnered resources using a combination of approaches—grant proposals, community partnerships, outside services. The collective eyes of the school were always alert for opportunities. Other important factors in these schools included participatory leadership emanating from the principal, teachers willing to take on greater responsibilities, a shared vision of school improvement, and the adequate training of all participants in SBM practices.

Joint Investigations

Similar to school systems in the studies noted above, higher-performing school districts in Texas (level one districts on the state's performance test) planned collaboratively within the district to find the means to address the needs of all students. A study of resource allocation practices and student achievement in Texas was undertaken by the Southwest Educational Development Laboratory (SEDL) in conjunction with the Charles A. Dana Center of the University of Texas at Austin. Their report stated that higher-performing districts used data, including student achievement outcomes, to identify specific needs. These districts often had instructional staff members and community representatives take part in district-level budget planning. Resources were generally allocated to schools using needs-based budgeting rather than set formulas for appropriations. And the higher-performing Texas districts were more inclined to reallocate funds when there was data to show that a change would produce improvement.

The Texas study noted that there was not a wide margin of difference in the traits between higher and lower performing districts. Nonetheless, the findings were strong enough for researchers to make an important distinction in their conclusion:

> Open and collaborative decision-making processes can be used to support improved student performance. In addition, the research suggests that school administrators who participate in data-driven, student-centered, and results-oriented budget processes may be able to make more effective use of resources than administrators who follow more rigid allocation formulas. (Alexander et al., 2000)

If done correctly, results-based budgeting can be a formidable force in the realization of improved levels of student achievement. It can also serve as a tool for lessening or eliminating wasteful spending on nonproductive materials or programs. This is especially so for programs that may be misaligned with district curricula and state standards, activities that show no measurable impact on socialization or achievement for the participating students. You've got to be able to freely and regularly raise questions about cost effectiveness: "If results promised from this effort are not being produced, must we continue to throw good money after bad?"

SCHOOL PERFORMANCE REVIEWS

A useful fiscal procedure that looks for the kind of information needed to effectively formulate cost-efficiency questions is the school performance review. A reliable aid in the search for answers to educational problems, performance reviews can be done from the vantage point of the individual school, the whole district, or both. In Missouri, for example, the state Department of Elementary and Secondary Education conducts performance reviews of school districts every five years. Under the Missouri School Improvement Plan, the review of districts focuses on the attainment of state education standards in order for the district to be awarded accreditation. The standards set by the state encompass the areas of school resources, processes, and performance.

In some states, school finances enter into performance reviews. Since 1991, the Texas State Comptroller's Office has conducted ongoing school performance reviews that include financial analyses. By 2002, 60 audits of Texas districts serving almost 1.5 million students had realized a total cost savings of about $600 million.

A large proportion of recommendations (90%) made by the Texas performance review teams are adopted by school systems. These recommendations often result in better school business practices. Similarly, in Florida each school district goes through a financial performance review every five years. Outside consultants contracted by Florida's Office of Program Policy Analysis and Government Accountability perform the reviews.

In Florida's Pinellas County school district, for example, the performance review process helped bring together a district budget committee. The mission of the budget committee is to keep spending priorities in line with anticipated resources, even during periods of budget crunches. Self-regulating expenditures and processes designed for budgetary stability and predictability help schools remain focused on their educational mission, to enable students to be successful.

Each year the practice of school performance reviews becomes more widespread. If your school is in a state that does not conduct regular performance reviews, there is no reason why a local school council or team at your site could not undertake its own analysis. Your school team could take a good look at achievement outcomes and weigh those outcomes against educational dollars invested. The performance-review practice would give your school its own set of useful data and establish a baseline year for analyzing trends. And you'd have a head start if evaluators should pay your school a visit or put your district under the performance-review microscope.

When performance reviews come into play, the traditional formula used for expressing school costs, per-pupil expenditures, takes a back seat to school productivity. When school costs are related to performance, student achievement scores, attendance and graduation rates, and persistence to completion of the educational program determine cost effectiveness. The job of schools is, and always has been, to educate students. Thus, costs are more logically calculated as the relationship between school resources and student outcomes. The formula for expressing school costs then becomes a ratio of resources to student attainment of targeted educational objectives. (See figure 1.1.)

Figure 1.1.   Site-Based Practices: A Typical Research Model

FINANCIAL FLEXIBILITY

Hand-in-hand with performance-review data, research repeatedly indicates that budget flexibility at the school site is an essential ingredient in the SBM script for success. As student data are regularly reviewed and analyzed, it may be necessary to reformulate instructional approaches. Funds are then redirected into particular curricular and instructional areas not envisioned as critical when the school's annual budget was initially finalized.

Schools are able to meet pressing needs as they arise if they have the on-site control to adjust already budgeted items. That is, the school budget committee needs the flexibility to redirect line-item funds already set aside for specific appropriations. They also need the authority to search out additional resources from outside sources. When internal district monies dry up, the ability to attract outside grants from government and private providers shows true budgetary power, a real indicator of flexibility at the school site.

STRAIGHTFORWARD COMMUNICATION

The delegation of resource-allocation decisions to the school level must not be ambiguous or convoluted. SBM lines of communication between central operations and the school site must remain open, clear, and forthright. Remember the 1967 movie *Cool Hand Luke*? The lead character, Lucas Jackson, is played by Paul Newman. Actor Strother Martin is the prison captain who admonishes Luke with the now-classic line: "What we've got here is a failure to communicate." Ironically, this is the same line that Luke, unbroken to the end, delivers as his last. Hopefully, this analogy is not appropriate to the organizational structure in your school district. At any rate, when there is a lack of communication, it will always contribute to misunderstandings between central administrators and school-site personnel. This can hamper or even destroy SBM effectiveness.

For example, 30 poorly performing districts in New Jersey were ordered by that state's highest court to adopt educational reforms in 1998. As designed, the program called for transferring resource-allocation procedures to the schools. The idea was that inclusive budgetary decision making by school councils and input from concerned parents and teachers would improve school effectiveness and performance. However, a study examined school-based budgeting in 57 schools in the 30 New Jersey districts and found that over the first two years of the program, implementation was weak.

During its first two years, site-based budgeting was rated unsatisfactory in New Jersey. Why? Several constraints were identified. Inconsistencies in communication between state and school personnel created problems. The lack of effective training in school budgetary procedures severely weakened implementation. Finally, "micromanagement" of affected schools by the state education bureaucracy threw a wrench into two-way communication and flexibility. In this case, micromanagement blocked the schools' abilities to place resources where they were warranted, at the time they were needed to deliver prescribed interventions designed to improve student learning.

The ability to avoid miscommunication also applies to information flowing from the schools to the central educational authority. When SBM is in place, participatory decision making to improve student achievement doesn't automatically mean that everyone in the school has a say. Nor does it mean that everything is decided at the school level, central administrators be hanged. A sound working equilibrium, a balance based on communication, collegiality, and flexibility, must be maintained between the school site and the central office. Establishing the necessary familiarity and trust, operating on the same wavelength, is an important component of the SBM relationship between central administrators and school-site staff, just as it is within the school.

A VIEW FROM THE LOCAL LEVEL

Case studies of SBM or its adaptations at the district and site level appear regularly in the literature. A few nuts-and-bolts issues are discussed here to give a general impression of past SBM efforts from around the nation. A historical perspective on SBM will help you plan for and implement the process in your own school or district. This knowledge base will contribute to an awareness of problems that could be encountered with site-based operations, especially those that involve fiscal control.

District or school personnel contemplating SBM should conduct an in-depth examination of site-based budgeting as implemented in systems similar to their own. It would seem advisable, too, that local investigative panels or action research teams study SBM in light of unique community priorities, rather than relying wholly on outside consultants or agencies for answers. What follows, then, may provide ideas about where to look to find data on a SBM system comparable in demographic and educational characteristics to your own district or school.

Boston

One example at the local level is the Boston (MA) public schools, a member of the Council of the Great City Schools. Boston formally assigned greater decision-making responsibilities to school sites with a citywide SBM initiative. Site decision-making practices surfaced in the district during 1992–93, when the Boston Teachers' Union in their contractual agreement bought into a plan that included SBM.

Teachers, parents, and site administrators composed Boston's school-site councils, who exercised some authority over hiring. Boston's goals were the same as those typically associated with SBM. That is, most school-related decisions are made at the school level. Quality and relevance of instruction are examined with an eye toward improvement. Collaborative efforts are focused on raising the achievement levels of all students. This includes the elimination of site practices that impede reform and delay the implementation of tested professional development activities. Boston schools received discretionary monies for supplies and staffing to meet individual school needs, but, as in many districts, constraints were attached to how those funds could be used. The Boston initiative had a SBM director in the central office assisting with and monitoring program implementation. Originally, site facilitators directed SBM professional development at each school; later, school council members delivered the training.

Finally, a major question connected with site-based efforts deals with student achievement. Was there any evidence of improved academic outcomes in Boston? Like other districts that implement SBM practices, a number of Boston's schools, but not all, showed increases on standardized test scores.

As with any educational endeavor, a limitation of decentralization is that it cannot automatically bring about improved academic outcomes across an entire school system. And when urban politicians and reform mayors view the public schools as a centerpiece in rebuilding their cities, as was the case in Boston, the pendulum may swing back toward a stronger central administration and a more "balanced" school system.

Seattle

A SBM district worth looking into, and a member of the Cross City Campaign discussed previously, is Seattle, WA. If every school district had a benefactor like Seattle's to fund its school transformation plans, site-based objectives might be put into place more smoothly—well, maybe.

In 2000, the Seattle public schools were awarded a $28 million grant over three years by the Bill and Melinda Gates Foundation. The goal is to transform all schools in the system. Each Seattle school received a one-year planning grant followed by two years of implementation monies. Similar to most SBM districts, a prime objective in Seattle is improved academic outcomes for all students and an end to disproportionate achievement associated with race, that is, a concerted effort to close the achievement gap.

As Seattle transitions toward becoming a standards-based system, its schools have moved into a decentralizing phase. The district has determined *what* the educational standards and grade-level benchmarks are, but, based on site needs, it's up to each school to figure out *how* to reach those goals. Operationally, this is called a "tight–loose philosophy." District guidelines are fixed, but each school has oversight of the development of its own instructional program. School leaders continually monitor implementation and outcomes and make necessary adjustments in light of district standards. Each school also controls its staff professional development, hiring procedures at the site, and a site-based budget that reflects the school's transformational plan.

Like other districts that apply SBM practices, funds in Seattle are apportioned to the schools with a weighted per-student formula. The formula takes into account total enrollment numbers, poverty levels of the families served by the school, and special instructional requirements at the site. This helps to establish a needs-based budgetary process. Roughly 100 schools in Seattle receive annual lump-sum allocations, including funds for selected staff and essential administrative costs.

Chicago

The extent of authority delegated to school councils to administer funds for personnel and to select staff members varies widely from district to district around the country. In Chicago, IL, for example, local school councils with staff selection powers functioned for more than 10 years at each of more than 500 sites. Councils included parents, community representatives, teachers, and the principal. The councils blazed the trail in school reform efforts. With the authority to develop budgets and review discretionary spending and yearly appropriations, they could request budget realignment from central administrators to meet school needs. Significantly, too, Chicago school councils selected and evaluated school principals and played a major role in designing school improvement plans.

Since the Chicago school reform law of the late 1980s, each school site theoretically shares equally in district funds. School councils realized a large measure of control over needs-based, states-apportioned monies, averaging half a million dollars per site. These funds are allocated on the proportion of low-income students who attend the school. Added to this is control over needs-based, federal Title 1 monies and whatever grants the schools were able to obtain to help in implementing instructional objectives.

Like Boston, however, the diminished control of the central office in Chicago didn't accomplish the great academic expectations hoped for in all schools. Possibly only one in three schools fashioned the necessary SBM team structure required to meet unique school needs. Once again, a "mayoral takeover" of the urban schools and a budget-minded leader for the district injected the missing factor in the Chicago equation, performance-based accountability.

Milwaukee

Following Chicago's lead, the Milwaukee, WI, schools initiated decentralization in the early 1990s. When the 160-plus Milwaukee schools began to let teachers and parents have more say in decisions affecting their schools, the central office started shifting greater responsibility for fund allocations to school sites. Funds for staff professional development, custodial services and supplies, and guidance counselors moved into the hands of the schools.

Thanks to concessions from the Milwaukee Teachers Education Association, some school governance teams could choose instructional staff without bowing to the rules of union seniority. However, this was not the case universally throughout the Milwaukee schools. And like most districts that undertake the move, the transition to school-based budgeting was not an easy one.

A significant lesson learned in Milwaukee schools is that principals who are able to make the necessary adjustments to SBM find that greater empowerment at the site is beneficial for everyone. Leadership styles may change, but leadership remains critical to the intent and task behind the school mission. Actually, in a SBM mode, the school principal requires more extensive and broader leadership capabilities than under a traditional centralized system.

In an examination of Milwaukee's move to school-based practices, one researcher noted, "How much flexibility principals can eke out of the new system depends on their experience, their skills, and their willingness to take risks" (Olson, 1997). Said another way, school leaders in a SBM environment must be able to adapt to changing circumstances. Rather than sticking firmly to established plans or old-line methods, those in the lead must take advantage of opportunities as they become apparent. In a well-functioning SBM environment, creativity counts.

St. Louis

Like Milwaukee, the St. Louis public schools (SLPS), the largest school system in Missouri, is a member of the Council of the Great City Schools. The City of St. Louis Board of Education, central administrators, and a team of principals studied SBM methods during the mid-1990s. In that process, guidance and constructive criticism were obtained from experts at the Mid-continent Regional Educational Laboratory (McREL) located in Colorado.

Following considerable review and discussion, a school-based management policy was initiated in St. Louis during 1996. And the concept has continued to evolve. The program, originally piloted at six sites, has expanded to scores of elementary, middle, and high schools, some of which face an ongoing struggle to make the transition.

In St. Louis, SBM was viewed as a way for schools and neighborhoods to come together and make decisions about education that directly affect them. Initially assisted by the district's SBM facilitator and other support staff, concerned principals and working councils now focus on ways to improve local school management on their own, albeit with uneven progress.

To give SBM a boost, St. Louis sought new ways to strengthen school leadership and address the recruitment, preparation, and support of principals. In 2002, the city's schools received a $5 million Wallace–Reader's Digest Leadership for Educational Achievement in Districts (LEAD) grant. Among numerous targeted objectives, St. Louis looked to integrate SBM with LEAD to further the concept of distributed leadership in the schools and work toward closing the achievement gap. A LEAD district team fashioned a strategic plan. The team focused on creating powerful learning communities of staff, students, and citizens around each school.

Similar to SBM districts throughout the nation, St. Louis school administrators anticipated that leadership development coupled with greater stakeholder involvement at the school level would strengthen innovations, accountability, and morale, and thus improve teaching, learning, and academic outcomes. From the inception of the program, the St. Louis Board of Education voiced an ongoing commitment "to empower principals, teachers, staff, students, parents and the community with the appropriate authority to work collaboratively to improve student achievement" (SLPS, n.d. [2002]).

Nevertheless, it seems that the answers to important questions have been left up to the individual schools. To some, the parameters of school empowerment may seem ambiguous. Principals ask: What is "appropriate authority"? How much of it has been given to my school? And how and by whom will appropriate authority be administered? The answers to these and other questions can place considerable influence in the hands of principals and their cohorts who participate on SBM councils, even with the constraints of outside federal, state, and district pressures.

Riding the educational teeter-totter and mirroring other urban school systems, the St. Louis public schools adjusted its focus on SBM in 2003. A greater measure of performance-based accountability was orchestrated from the central office. It's hard to keep politics out of public education. In St. Louis, a mayor's slate of school board candidates won election and contracted with a corporate management team to restructure the school system.

GARNERING FUNDS AND GATHERING RESOURCES

Regardless of the context of national, state, and local political circumstances, principals in the know can use the techniques of SBM to their school's advantage. Together with school leadership teams, they can enhance site-controlled fiscal practices to acquire resources that beef up school services or plug the holes in shrinking budgets. Integral to school success in these areas is a detailed understanding of school financial practices.

Table 1.1 lists some positive and negative factors associated with resource acquisitions and appropriations using SBM. The list doesn't show all the elements, which span a complex, multidimensional framework. Keep in mind that school systems adjust SBM to various formats.

Table 1.1.   SBM Strengths and Weaknesses

SBM Strengths	SBM Weaknesses
• Diffused power and accountability spreads financial know-how and resource management throughout the school, beyond just a few site leaders. • Shared on-site budget review and resource allocation heightens staff members' understanding of school needs, improving team resolve to find solutions to problems. • Guarded management of resources limits divergent programs and contributes to instructional program coherence. • Community awareness of individual school finances lends support to districtwide initiatives and bond issues. • Creativity in accessing worthwhile resources is acknowledged and rewarded. • Unique school needs are identified and funds are appropriated where they will do the most good for students.	• Ambiguity in board of education or central-office delegation of authority can confuse and limit site fiscal management efforts. • Extensive training in budget management and fiscal practices, beyond instructional leader and school manager roles, is required for real efficiency. • District turf wars, mandated programs, and on-site pet projects create roadblocks to effectively using possible resource providers. • Activating joint staff member, parent, and community member participation to discuss financial issues on councils, subcommittees, or ad-hoc groups takes much time and effort. • Loss of key staff members weakens fiscal management. • Mandated SBM rarely works without meaningful training or the ability to customize resource acquisition to school needs.

* Adapted from Kedro (2003).

Also, an innovative principal and school staff may be using pieces of SBM, perhaps under some other name, to achieve resource-acquisition success in a district that doesn't necessarily advocate on-site control.

EDUCATION RESEARCH A "MAGIC BAG"?

Picture a kindergarten teacher amusing kids with a game called Magic Bag (please, *not* Arnold Schwarzenegger in *Kindergarten Cop*).* The teacher reaches into a sack and shouts, "What you see is what you get!" Out pop treats—little prizes for lessons well learned. Sometimes magic tricks surface from the bag, and all marvel at the teacher's sleight of hand. With a sheepish grin, the teacher might even come up empty-handed. Reward or reproof, we're never certain what we'll see next. But whatever is pulled from the bag gets the kids' attention.

Could education research be mistaken for a game of Magic Bag? Reach in, grab some data, and remember, "What you see is what you get." But not always.

To begin, you'd think superior schools and superb teachers improve student achievement. If our input is excellent, our outcome should be no less, right? Not exactly. The Magic Bag of the 1960s and 1970s found that teachers, books, supplies, or facilities little influenced student outcomes. Resources didn't do much for test scores. That research, still telling, says academic payoffs rest heavily on student traits and family status.

If recognized schooling inputs don't have much impact, are they ignored? Certainly not. Grab a treat from the bag. In the late 1970s and 1980s, researchers found "effective schools." Effective schools benefit impoverished kids and challenge the pessimism that attaches itself to public education. Today we hear much about "accelerated schools" or schools practicing all variety of instructional reform models. Deprived children, it's said, show higher achievement in these schools than might be anticipated by their circumstances.

Agreement was never unanimous that traditional inputs do little for academic outcomes. Likewise, "effective schools" had performed well for many decades before being discovered in the 1970s. Put another

---

* This section is adapted from Kedro (1993).

way, some research snubs school resources in judging student attainments. Other research bemoans the lack of those same resources in our schools.

Research susceptibility to Tweedledum and Tweedledee blurs its practicality. In the 1980s, a U.S. assistant secretary for educational research said, "Our field has not yet succeeded in persuading many people that education research is valuable or worthwhile." In the 1990s, a New Jersey judge ruled, "The existing education research is relatively primitive and does not reveal very much about student learning." Others say research is a delaying tactic, postponing actions that could improve education and direct needed resources to students.

Regardless, schools don't thrive nourished just on research. So why are we so often mesmerized by reports that say U.S. public schools are in jeopardy and our students at risk? Lately, studies of poor teacher training and inequalities among school systems sowed more despair. When the media highlight only public education's shortcomings, the magic bag leaves us emptyhanded.

Is education research a guidepost or an afterthought? "We are either part of the problem or part of the solution," say the education reformers. Out of the magic bag comes an old charm. Schooling is not solely the responsibility of one group—not teachers, parents, students, or communities acting in isolation. "If everything [in education] went wrong," a university president has said, "for everything to go right, more than just the schools will need to go right—all of American society."

"Going right" happens one step at a time. In this instance, another program comes to mind—school-based management and site-based budgeting. Teachers, school administrators, concerned citizens, business leaders, parents, students, and neighborhoods can work together to define the school mission and improve student achievement. Then the research becomes what you make of it.

After the research is said and done, maybe the best measure of any school is the commitment of everyone closest to it. Properly implemented school-based practices might help to accomplish positive academic outcomes. As one educator put it, "Strong families, small schools, and old-fashioned values give us education money can't buy."

CHAPTER 1 SUMMARY

The SBM team in your district or school can conduct its own review of relevant research. They can expand on topics discussed above or look into areas that may be more appropriate to your school's particular needs. Obviously, you can't plan in a vacuum. But neither should you swallow hook, line, and sinker all of the information that you'll cast about for and reel in while you design your SBM program.

With that in mind, let's review some primary concepts behind SBM that you should remember from your trip along the research road. If you like, you can take your own journey into the literature and build on these ideas. In doing so, you may add details you deem important to your school system, possibly even create a horse of a different color.

First, site-based fiscal management is not for everyone. It requires extensive training and long-term commitment from key participants. And while on-site budgetary control is a star in the SBM script, other elements need to be in place as well. These include managerial ability, access to information, and rewards for performance. The focus of SBM is on improved student achievement, not merely restructuring so that all the players can have a larger or louder voice in school affairs.

Second, SBM seems to work best when school personnel evidence some degree of entrepreneurial spirit, intrinsic motivation, and self-direction. School staff are able to overcome roadblocks and find resources on their own, and they are rewarded for their efforts. The goal of securing resources is part of the larger pursuit of ideas that advance results-oriented instructional change in the school.

Third, SBM systems are data-driven, flexible, and needs-based. Information gained from school performance reviews identifies student strengths and weaknesses, uncovers any lack of effectiveness in the instructional program, and targets areas for appropriate intervention to improve academic outcomes. The power to adjust the school's needs-based budget and to seek and secure outside resources—flexibility at the site—is critical.

Finally, communication between central administrators and school-site personnel must be open, clear, and based on a shared philosophy. Leaders at the school need to be skilled in adapting to change and taking risks to create opportunities. They must be able to capitalize on the acquisition of resources when they become available.

CHAPTER 1 REFLECTION AND DISCUSSION

1. On a personal level, how would school-based management (SBM) benefit you as an educator? Is SBM an issue open to discussion in your school? In your district? Why or why not?

2. What are some school systems in your state, or perhaps across the nation, that have characteristics similar to yours (e.g., enrollment and racial/ethnic makeup, total dollar-amount budgets, per-pupil expenditures, number of school sites and staff, pupil/teacher ratios)? Among these school systems, which use some form of SBM or site-based budgeting? How are they faring in standardized student achievement outcomes compared to your school and district?

3. Is there a teacher team or informal group in your school involved in action research? Have they investigated SBM concepts at the school level with an eye toward resource acquisitions, innovative instructional strategies, and improved student achievement? Would they be interested in taking on such a project? Could you do a preliminary ERIC search on the topic and share it with them to generate interest?

4. What do the principal and site administrators at your school think about SBM strategies? Have budget allocations, acquisitions planning, or instructional resource needs assessments come up for discussion in your school staff meetings? Could such concepts be placed on school staff meeting agendas by concerned grade-level or subject-area teacher teams?

5. What is a school performance review, and how would your school go about conducting one?

6. Could your district's central-office administrators, or a coalition of teachers chosen to represent your district's schools, apply for a grant to study the feasibility of adopting/adapting SBM budgeting methods at selected sites in your district?

7. What schools in your district, do you think, would be most adept at piloting school-based budgeting? On what criteria did you base your selection?

CHAPTER 2

School-Based Financial Planning

"It's enough that we're letting him work to support the flock of us. He can't have everything." That's how the family sees Father in the rollicking film musical about the 1904 World's Fair, *Meet Me in St. Louis!* (1944). Actor Leon Ames plays Alonzo "Lon" Smith, the father who has a hard time keeping up with family matters. To lessen the chances of confrontation, Lon is kept in the dark about things that might upset him, including certain items in the family's expense account. In one scene, Father firmly puts his foot down: "I'm curious, just when was I voted out of this family?"

Like a smooth-running family, a well-organized school has mechanisms in place to see to it that everyone is informed about pertinent fiscal matters as well as instructional and achievement issues. Opinions are heard and considered. It's understood that plans may not turn out right if key members of the family are left in the dark. The same generally holds true for school-based budgeting.

School-based budgeting denotes the place where decision making and control of the budget planning process occur. Budget control at the school site may or may not be a feature of school-based management (SBM). Budget planning centered in the school involves shared fiscal decision making. School staff members identify instructional and learning needs across subject areas, grade levels, and classrooms. Remember, school-based budgeting is not the complete decentralization of district financial procedures; Father is not left out of the family circle. That step might contribute to gross inefficiencies in districtwide financial management. It would surely lessen the power of numbers in purchasing. It could also disrupt the coherence of districtwide programs. Legal and business services, capital expenditures, transportation and maintenance, and non-instructional functions are more efficiently handled at the district level.

There are district resources, however, that can be allocated to the school site. SBM, effectively implemented, can improve school-level efficiency and productivity. Overcoming inefficiencies in the distribution of funds to schools and improving the response time required to redirect those funds can be one benefit derived from school-based budgeting.

The public, teachers' organizations, and government policy makers sometimes contend that the resources reaching the classroom to improve teaching and learning are only a small fraction of the total school-district budget. Public schools, especially in urban areas, are painted as heavily bureaucratic, inefficient, and without sound performance standards. Research, however, generally shows that urban districts allocate a smaller proportion of expenditures to administration than do other systems. Poorer urban districts also spend more on teachers' salaries relative to expenditures for support staff than do many nonurban school systems.

Nonetheless, criticism continues to be directed at fiscal waste and academic mediocrity in public education. For example, a political science professor at the University of Missouri–St. Louis authored a book that attacks many current trends in K–12 education. His efforts are a crusade in what he calls the "Great American Education War." The professor sees two basic problems in today's schools: a "dumbing down of academics" and a movement of resources away from traditional, rigorous learning standards into the social domains of school parenting, self-esteem building, character education, and the like (Rochester, 2002).

One response to these problems in public education, which in many instances may be legitimate concerns, could lie in school-based budgeting. When reliably performed, shared fiscal management can be a strong measure aimed at dispelling misperceptions about a school's standards and the use of its funds. State laws often explicitly spell out accountability measures to citizens as the foundation of budgeting and fiscal reporting. School-based budgeting can provide diverse stakeholders with the opportunity to look more closely at how resources are allocated at the school site. Stakeholders can see for themselves if the application of those funds contributes to improved student achievement and public education excellence. If not, they can do something about it.

A community that supports its schools has a right to know what educational results they can expect and when they can anticipate seeing these results. Citizens also want to know what measures will be taken to provide tangible rewards for accomplishments and what sanctions will be imposed for continued lack of improvement. Accountability from site administrators and teachers is usually embedded in the site-based budgeting process.

The underpinnings of sound school financial management include budgetary comprehensiveness and discipline. The budget presents all of the fiscal operations that enter into decisions related to academic performance against a backdrop of the extent of allocations, constraints, and demands that affect the school site. Fiscal discipline dictates that the budget will employ resources economically, using only the resources required to accomplish the school mission and using them wisely. Efforts are made to minimize program and political biases that could adversely impact effective implementation and positive outcomes.

Decisions made during the budget process must be linked to district policies, especially those that define the educational outcomes sought for students. Fiscal decision-making calls for flexibility in assembling and weighing all relevant information coupled with site authority for program decisions. In turn, the efficient implementation of school programs demands attention to the balance between short-term and long-term goals. The school budgetary approach should allow for adjustment to programmatic imbalances and quick response to evaluations of instructional practice and assessments of student achievement. Finally, accurate and understandable reporting of school costs, programs, and results emanating from the above procedures should be communicated to the public in a timely manner.

VARIATIONS OF SITE-BASED BUDGETING

The handling of school finances under SBM can take many forms. For example, Lawler (as cited by Wohlstetter & Mohrman, 1996) reports that school-based budgeting within a "high involvement framework" presents an ideal situation. It gives true budgetary power to stakeholders at the school site. This seldom occurs, however, because four primary domains of authority must shift from the central office to the schools.

In a high-involvement scenario, the SBM governing body controls staff recruitment and selection, substitute teacher and utility expenses, the source of services and supplies, and the carryover of unspent money from year to year (G. Hentschke, as cited in Wohlstetter & Mohrman, 1996). This is not the case in many SBM districts. Most schools don't even want to deal with utilities. And when a district is composed of a large number of schools challenged by relatively high rates of staff turnover and student mobility, as most schools in urban districts are, appropriate centralized fiscal oversight is imperative. Research says that rarely do schools receive "real" on-site control of all budgetary allocations.

Perhaps a more realistic aim of on-site authority is to provide individual schools with the ability to redirect particular resources. In this SBM scenario, discretionary funds are used to support identified needs that can best accomplish improved student achievement at the site. Certainly, staff recruitment and selection is at the forefront of quality teaching and improved achievement. For example, in the St. Louis public schools and in other medium sized to large districts, principals have a degree of input in this area. But personnel stipulations from the central office and the teachers' union also play a role, as they do in most systems. Rarely do on-site decision makers have direct control over teacher salaries and benefits, which account for the bulk, often 90% or more, of education expenditures. So where is the on-site fiscal control?

School systems in Denver, CO; Milwaukee, WI; Rochester, NY; and St. Louis, MO, have discretionary funds within their budgets based on districtwide ratios and allocation rules. In many SBM districts, site-controlled discretionary items relate primarily to security and custodial staff overtime, custodial supplies, day-to-day substitutes (*not* continuing substitute teachers), and parent involvement activities. However, if school-site savings accumulate, funds must be expended within the district's business calendar year; there is no year-to-year carryover. This is a hurdle, but effective SBM principals and teams take it in stride. To do so, it's imperative that productive plans are in place and sound alternatives already in mind to use funds when they become available.

Site-based budgeting requires that tentative instructional ideas and proposals be defined and laid out on paper, ready to go. These plans represent worthwhile strategies that have been investigated by school staff members. The planned methods are believed to be effective for addressing student needs. Tentative plans can be quickly reevaluated and implemented as new funds come to light in the school budget or as monies flow into the school from outside sources.

THE BUDGET PLANNING CYCLE

The direction that your school's budget planning process takes will depend in large measure on the levels of fiscal authority turned over to your school management team. Are you able to work within a high-involvement script or must you play a smaller, more restrained role? Whatever the degree of autonomy at the site, whatever the limitations placed on your fiscal responsibility, it's critical to link school needs with the school improvement plan and the school budget.

School needs, targeted improvements, and available resources should not be viewed as separate and isolated issues. Preparing the paperwork that defines these matters should not be performed perfunctorily. Rather, planning should be approached as a cyclical, ongoing process. School budget team members should see fiscal planning to meet academic needs as vital to the mission of educating students. The budget process, then, becomes an ongoing exercise that comprises preparing, evaluating, revising, and reporting. (See figure 2.1.)

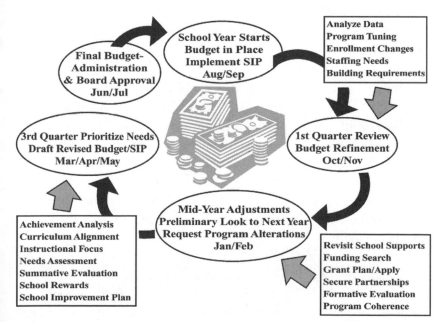

Figure 2.1. Assess Needs, Plan Improvement, Budget: An Interactive Cyclical Process

The School Needs Assessment

Begin thinking about the school budget by performing a comprehensive site needs assessment. The needs assessment determines strengths and weaknesses in student learning and instructional delivery. With this information, learning objectives and staff professional development can be targeted to breach gaps in both student skills and teacher competencies at the school. With accurate needs assessment data, professional development can be tied directly to student learning, which should ultimately result in improved achievement. Considerable published material is available that provides specific, helpful directions in designing and conducting a school needs assessment (e.g., U.S. Dept. of Education, 1998). These studies should be consulted before beginning your school's site-based plan to restructure resources toward improved academic outcomes.

Needs assessment data assembled and analyzed creates a snapshot of the school. Beginning points to examine are school enrollment, pupil/teacher ratios, and per-pupil expenditures. Areas in the school profile that focus on students may include achievement outcomes obtained on national and state standardized assessments and district-developed tests. Student attendance rates, persistence to completion or graduation rates, ACT/SAT average scores, and various percentages for student mobility, those qualified for free and reduced lunch, grade-level retention, suspension/expulsion, and the like, are helpful in painting a picture of the school's achievement patterns and demographics.

School profile information can be used to examine the alignment of the school's curriculum and instruction with district and state standards. It also can describe the availability, participation, and use of worthwhile professional development opportunities, the participation of parent and community members in school programs, and the overall level of satisfaction of teachers, students, and parents with the school climate or culture.

Gathering, analyzing, synthesizing, and accurately reporting the above data categories is time consuming. Therefore, it's important that your data collection tools are clear and easy to use. If the school team has developed its own instrument package, you may wish to pilot test it with a small sample group in order to resolve any problems before using it on a wide scale. Wherever practicable, individuals collecting and analyzing the data should assure contributors that their responses will be kept confidential.

Data collection should focus on obtaining the information most important to the mission of your school. Needs assessment planning should ensure ease of collection, relevance of information, and reliability of the data. Different stakeholders in the school should have an opportunity for input through surveys, interviews, or focus groups. However, don't waste the time of school staff members and those responding to surveys with unnecessary questions or with long and tedious interview procedures. If the data gathered are too complex, your focus on critical issues in the analysis and reporting phase may become bogged down or drift off center. You don't want to miss the mark of what is truly essential to the school's needs.

After the data are gathered, tabulated, and disseminated, school staff members on the SBM team and on grade-level or subject-area teacher teams can analyze and interpret the needs assessment. They can use it to prepare plans for improving curriculum and instruction that will meet high academic standards. You might even call together discussion groups comprising teachers, parents, or students to review critical needs assessment information and become better informed about school issues. Time spent on data analysis can be thought of as the beginning phase of self-study, a continuous process of reexamination in the school.

When we use reliable indicators and outcome measures, the perceptions of school staff, that is, what we think is happening based on our day-to-day observations in the school, are tempered, qualified, adjusted, or confirmed. The needs assessment, the hard data, becomes the driving force behind making decisions, planning programs, and allocating resources.

In summary, the needs assessment provides for the systematic collection and analysis of pertinent data that will connect attainment of the school's goals to the needs of the school. A comprehensive needs assessment is the basis upon which the school improvement plan can be built. It also identifies critical areas where possible expenditures will be required to meet those needs. Priorities can be set and objectives formalized to accomplish the academic standards required by the Board of Education and the state.

The School Improvement Plan

The school improvement plan (SIP) is a set of long-range goals that your school management team creates and writes based upon school needs and ongoing self-evaluations of staff development and student performance. The SIP promotes continuous growth. The process of creating and following the SIP helps to establish a goal-oriented and results-driven school culture. The interaction of data analysis and assessment to reach short-term results may produce long-term gains in student achievement. Included in the SIP are specific actions that will be taken to improve academic outcomes and close the gaps in student achievement. These anticipated outcomes will be completed over a set period of time, usually three to five years.

The SIP should be thought of as a working plan that is subject to regular review and annual adjustment. Your school's SIP is a document separate from the districtwide improvement plan, which generally defines how the district will help the schools. However, your SIP must be congruent with your district's goals. The SIP incorporates the district's mission, which is built on the state's educational standards and benchmarks. The SIP sets measurable school targets to reach those educational goals. Broad goals have one or more specific objectives that must be attained, and the objectives may be tied to several instructional strategies or learning activities that will be applied to produce the desired results.

The SIP addresses the unique requirements of the school. It defines the individual school mission and assembles the school-level strategies and tactics that will be implemented to attain the academic outcomes. The SIP can be viewed as a series of linked actions, perhaps four or five primary programs functioning in congruence, not disparately applied, that school staff will put into motion to get the job of educational excellence done.

The SIP presents a unified direction for improvement that school staff members agree to embark upon. Developing and writing the plan might be one of the responsibilities of the SBM team or it could be delegated to a separate school improvement team. In any case, administrators and teachers who make up the SIP team must be able to reach consensus and should be in close touch with the entire school community in order to design an appropriate strategic direction and avoid omissions. The team should have a good working relationship and regular interaction with school staff members so that minor revisions to the SIP, if necessary to accomplish objectives, can be successfully introduced during the school year.

With the district mission statement and goals to serve as guidelines, the SIP team uses the findings from the school's needs assessment to engage in dialogue. Data-driven study by the team identifies requirements for student and staff improvements. Your school's SIP team develops a mission statement that describes the purpose and function of your school, whom your school serves, and how the services provided by your school meet the unique needs of your school's student population.

The SIP team will produce the school mission statement, then identify objectives or targets aligned with accomplishing that mission. Each target has a strategy and list of tactics. All of the above elements are aligned in support of district goals. The SIP usually includes a series of school program descriptors within a hierarchical arrangement. For example, one format might descend from goals to objectives to activities to outcomes, and define how the outcomes are to be evaluated.

SIP objectives, or targets, are defined for both student achievement and staff development. For example, targets tell what the students will do to demonstrate their level of performance. One of the targets might be a particular schoolwide percentage increase that has been realistically determined and is obtainable on the state assessment in communication arts or mathematics. Teacher expectations might be the completion of training and the infusion of proven classroom methods to improve student receptivity to learning. Staff development should be targeted in curricular areas of greatest need.

SIP strategies are the comprehensive plans; tactics are the actions that will be taken to achieve those plans. Activities can describe the specific steps that will be done to show that the processes to obtain the outcomes are in place. Measurable outcomes, or benchmarks, provide for the longitudinal analyses of trends to see if the objectives are being accomplished.

For example, a research-based, balanced literacy program could be a strategy; its tactics might be the training of K–3 teachers in methods that employ a combination of phonics and literature. Some of the activities, observable in the classroom, would be using phonics to improve reading and spelling (e.g., word walls), cooperative-learning literature circles, retelling stories to assess comprehension, and teaching and assessing process writing. Measurable outcomes could be the teachers' running records of student growth in classroom communication arts projects. Trend analyses of student achievement could use classroom and school-wide change in language arts scores as shown on a national standardized test or a state performance assessment.

All of the above facets are examined by the SBM and/or SIP teams. The data are used to evaluate the degree of implementation of the balanced literacy intervention and to determine the extent of its effect on student achievement. Other objectives in the SIP are delineated and evaluated in the same way.

There are a variety of helpful sources to give direction in preparing the SIP and analyzing its effects. Your school system will likely have its own set of guidelines and a standard SIP format. For additional SIP ideas, templates, and calendars, the education departments of the states of Rhode Island and Maryland are among several that share useful materials on the Internet (Rhode Island, 1999–2003; Maryland, n.d.). A systematic process for analyzing a SIP in order to maximize improvement efforts, prioritize tasks, and focus resources has been developed by Sweeny (1997) and is also available on the Internet.

Finally, as the SIP is examined at different times of the school year, questions are asked that relate to budgetary matters as well as to achievement outcomes and staff professional development. To what degree is each objective in the SIP being accomplished? Are the levels of implementation for each objective and the results that it produces in student achievement worth the investment? That is, is each program cost effective? These questions are directly linked to budgetary matters. The list that follows is a complete set of guiding questions for using a needs assessment when creating an improvement plan and budget:

- What *exactly* do you want to accomplish at your school? What are your vision and goals?
- Who will constitute the SBM team? Will the team include the principal, lead teachers, Title 1 teachers, instructional support staff, parents, members of the community, students?
- Who will be charged with planning, implementing, and monitoring the school needs assessment?

- What is your system for gathering and analyzing data? What kinds of data (standardized achievement tests, student attendance and behavior data, teacher/parent/student surveys, communitywide input measures) will you use? Are you selective in choosing only essential data focused on pertinent questions, useful information that is easily collected?
- Have you established baselines, beginning measures taken from the data in each of your school's areas of concern from which to see trends toward improvement?
- Have new questions arisen along the way? Is any important information missing from your initial assessment, and how will you get it?
- Have you prepared a report based on the needs assessment, showing data categories and explaining findings and recommendations in easily understood text, tables, and graphics? Are the objectives in the report meaningful and aligned with district and state standards?
- Has the SBM team thoroughly digested the needs assessment and prepared the annual school improvement plan in response to critical academic needs? Have specific instructional and learning objectives been spelled out in the SIP, expressing in detail the measurable improvements sought and how and when they will be accomplished?
- Has the SBM team or site-based budget committee used the needs assessment and SIP to plan the budget? Is the budget aligned with academic needs and targeted objectives so that appropriated and discretionary funds are used within a coherent instructional program?
- Has the SIP and budget planning process incorporated resource acquisition goals in grant planning, fundraising, partnerships, and other outside sources directed at accomplishing the school's instructional mission?

The School Budget

The school budgeting process flows out of the needs assessment and throughout the school improvement plan. The budget is intertwined with both needs and improvement. The needs assessment helps to identify the goals and objectives that will guide the school and can be viewed as one piece in budget planning. The SIP defines the curriculum, instruction, and programs that will be implemented to accomplish the school's goals and objectives. The budget tells everyone when and where the money is coming from and how and to whom the money is going.

Site-based budget decision makers, depending on the number of items in the budget over which they have control, gain the advantage of placing funds where they believe the most good will be done for students. While great care must be exercised in decentralizing budgetary authority, responsibility for results devolves to the site. This process contributes to greater staff and parent participation. Stakeholders in the school have the opportunity to be involved in budget preparation and maintenance. School staff are not merely implementing the budget after the central office creates it or the Board of Education authorizes it. But remember, with increased control comes greater accountability.

Accountability means that the budget is reviewed for its effectiveness in accomplishing school objectives regularly throughout the school year. Planning and preparing the school budget is not a one-shot exercise. The budget, like the implementation of the school's instructional program, requires evaluation. Budgetary evaluation is an ongoing study of how monies were expended and if the expenditures achieved results in improving student achievement. Assessing expenditures also demonstrates accountability in balancing the budget—what comes in goes out. And if carryover of particular funds is possible, evaluation makes known all reserve funds that are in place for specified future allocations.

The essence of budgetary evaluation is that the SBM team is accountable to the school and its stakeholders for getting the job done, that is, for effectively educating all of the students. The process of evaluating and reporting finances shows that resources were obtained and used properly, in compliance with district, state, and federal requirements. It also shows whether the school's resources were adequate to cover the costs of the educational services provided. Finally, it helps the site budget committee assess program cost effectiveness.

BUDGETARY APPROACHES

The budgetary process used by your school will be influenced by the type of budget that is in place in the district. A variety of budget formats are used by school systems. Your hard copy or electronic budget format is the vehicle that moves your school from the realm of educational policy into the spheres of financial planning and program execution.

Generally, school districts use one of several basic budgetary approaches: (1) line-item budgeting, (2) performance budgeting, (3) program-planning budgeting, (4) zero-based budgeting, or (5) outcome budgeting. Often, site-based budgeting is viewed as another distinct type among the above formats. Regardless, a structured budgetary approach delineating district-controlled and school-controlled finances will be used by your school for accounting purposes. The type of budget employed could be district-mandated or, in some instances, may even represent an amalgamation of the above approaches that best meets the needs of your district or school.

Line-Item Budget

Line-item budgeting is the traditional approach used by many school systems. The budget is developed using historical funding and expenditure references. For example, the school's computer lab appropriation would be determined from the previous year's allocation. Adjustments may be made for inflation, systemwide cutbacks, or other fiscal and cost-effectiveness considerations. All expenditures are lined up and submitted to the central office and the board for approval. Funds are then appropriated to the school for the line-item amounts.

The line-item process, however, is highly structured and controlled. It doesn't allow leeway at the school site for quick budget modification and redirection of funds to meet newly identified academic needs. Budgetary change requires approval from the central administration or board. Since this takes considerable time and effort, it's often seen as a drawback of the line-item process. Moreover, the line-item budget may focus too heavily on the allocation of funds at the expense of ongoing examination of long-term goals directed at improving achievement outcomes.

Performance Budget

Performance budgeting moves beyond the line-item budget to provide a descriptive outline of school programs and services in organizational units, and what those programs are supposed to achieve. In some cases, performance budgeting may be incorporated into aspects of line-item budgeting. Budget amounts are derived from either standard unit costs or, more likely in schools, historical costs for a particular service.

For example, a school consumer science and family planning program may be budgeted based on the extent of activities, materials, and outcomes sought compared to past expenditure levels for that program and its accomplishments. The performance budget is planned and built on cost estimates for delivering school activities and services with a focus on outcomes. Strictly speaking, however, the performance budget does not assess the degree to which the described programs and services are the correct ones for achieving the district's or school's long-range educational goals.

Program-Planning Budget

Program-planning budgeting (PPB) differs from the above budgetary applications in that it looks toward long-range goals. PPB is more global in perspective and subject to fewer strict limitations on its approach. The PPB plan may be a proposal or report that centers on main programs designed to achieve the school's goals rather than focusing on the detailed specifics presented in the line-item budget. Essential educational objectives are identified and all program costs are connected to these objectives in the school's long-range plan.

For example, data are assembled on students, services, staffing, facilities, and finances; questions are then posed around how many, how much, when, where, and what will be done to reach the school's long-range goals. While this procedure puts greater emphasis on the accomplishment of the school's mission, it requires strong analytical ability in financial projections and accounting techniques, cohesiveness across programs, and consensus on the fundamental objectives of the school.

Zero-Based Budget

Zero-based budgeting (ZBB) is time consuming and data intensive. All school programs and services are reviewed and prioritized. Budget planners cost out all school needs for the coming school year. Everything is ranked by the degree to which it contributes to producing the results required to reach the school's set outcomes. ZBB presents all school activities in the order of their assessed importance. This approach allows for the removal of low-priority programs, and when spending cuts are required, it directs decisions about which programs will stay. ZBB concentrates resources where they'll do the most good.

For example, your school's annual evaluation of support programs may determine that an instructional model is low on the totem pole. If the program hasn't measured up in attaining sought-after academic outcomes, its service providers are eliminated from the next year's budget. However, a thorough evaluation of all programs is required for ZBB, and this is laborious. Moreover, in certain cases, state or federal mandated services need to be retained regardless of their priority or your school's needs.

Outcome Budget

Outcome budgeting contains elements of all of the above approaches. As its name implies, outcome budgeting ties the appropriation of funds to the creation of useful outcomes. School resources are assigned to those activities and providers that utilize the resources to the school's best advantage. When outcomes are the centerpiece of budget planning, goals and objectives have been identified and well defined. Budgeted funds are directly linked to meeting those objectives and producing the desired outcomes. Accomplishing the school mission predominates over all other issues.

Outcome budgeting calls for the preparation of indicators. The indicators of input and output are the resources applied and the things produced. For example, input indicators in a school computer program could be the number of computers in the school and the amount of student access time. Output indicators could be the number of students who successfully master keyboarding, word processing, or Internet research skills. The outcome indicators identify and explain the results of the computer program and its effectiveness, that is, the change measured in student performance in producing or presenting quality, inquiry-based products. Efficiency indicators tell the cost per unit to obtain the output, or the cost-effectiveness of the program.

Research finds that an organizational structure fashioned around an outcome budget approach has benefits attached to it. In the world of government bureaucracy, for example, studies indicate that outcome budgeting promotes improved efficiency, more innovations, increased flexibility, and higher staff morale, all leading to greater effectiveness in attaining results.

Cash Management

Whatever the budgetary process or combination of approaches used by your school, it's imperative that a cash management policy is in place and consistently monitored. The control of monies under the cash management policy is usually in the hands of the principal, but a designee with the skills and responsibility to handle the task could be appointed. Nonetheless, the principal is ultimately responsible for the funds. School-site funds falling within the cash management plan are usually assigned within broad categories such as materials and supplies, student activities, parent involvement functions, and capital or equipment funds.

For example, under materials and supplies in the cash management plan, there is often a petty cash fund for purchases of an immediate nature limited to small dollar amounts. A separate set of books should be kept for the petty cash fund. The collection and spending of user fees for school activities should be recorded and monitored in a similar fashion. Receipts should be provided for all incoming fees, and the funds collected should be spent only on the activities for which they are designated.

Larger material expenditures require a purchase order for prior approval. This process should be efficiently designed and understood by all of the staff at the school in order to avoid bottlenecks. Each school purchase requires tracking that specifies the exact amount spent, by whom, when, and on what. A general ledger, a standardized method of entries somewhat like a checkbook, records each expenditure. Transactions can be encoded using the school-district fund, function, and object numbers. The transactions are usually entered on a personal computer and electronically submitted to the central office for collection, consolidation, and review. Most often, the principal has the responsibility for seeing to it that these matters of record keeping and submission are performed properly and in a timely manner.

A Budgetary Tale of Two Schools

Two public schools located in the "gateway to the west" were spotlighted by the press. Let's call the schools City High and County High. Ironically, at different times, both schools achieved either fiscal fame or fiscal notoriety—saint to sinner or sinner to saint.

Fiscal matters in County High first caught the public's attention years ago when it made the six o'clock news. Its principal, juggling the books for who knows how long, had pilfered school funds (textbook accounts, student programs, vending machines). Perhaps tens of thousands of dollars were skimmed into personal accounts. (SBM budgetary oversight, had it been in place, might have checked this criminal activity.)

At the time County High was meeting its fiscal demise, City High was transforming itself into a magnet program. Restructured City High attracted students and received increased funding. It pulled outside resources into its much-praised educational venue. City's future looked rosy.

Years passed and roles reversed. Now City High found itself in the public stocks. An auditing firm delivered its annual report to the school board on issues of finance and compliance. Among shortcomings, auditors discovered $7,000 in cash withdrawals unaccounted for in City High's funds. Its books had not been reconciled for two years and its fiscal methods were deemed inadequate.

What had gone wrong? Perhaps City's principal relied too much on the school bookkeeper. Purchases had not been properly documented. The bookkeeper couldn't recall the cash withdrawals. He said he had only followed orders, and anyway, he planned to resign at the end of the school year. The principal declined to comment and deferred answers to the main office.

Other problems surfaced at City High that indicated a lack of budgetary planning. The school ordered 250 yearbooks in excess of student demand; it was stuck for $6,000. Another $2,000 showed up in bounced checks received by the school, monies not recovered by either the school or the main office. At any rate, City High promptly prohibited staff from using cash withdrawals to pay for school purchases.

County High, on the other hand, now entered the limelight. It had created and courted an alumni association. It encouraged graduates to consider school needs. Efforts to cultivate outside resources paid off. A prosperous alumnus gave $1 million for a new student commons. The early-1960s graduate recalled the benefits bestowed by his alma mater. He noted much had changed since he left high school, but he hit upon a constant—educated youth pave the way to a better future. His gift, gratefully received, was dedicated to the entire school community. Students would have a hand in advising on the interior design, colors, and furnishings for their commons, an impossible dream come true thanks to fundraising efforts.

Is there a moral to this tale of two schools? Yes. Without fiscal controls, your school can be riding high one day and in the tank the next. Those who oversee school finances, whether SBM is in place or not, can never be too careful. Practicing sound record keeping, retaining accountability for *all* resources, and securing some of those resources from outside the system are central to site-based budgeting.

FISCAL TRAINING

At the site level, financial awareness involves a principal's direct or shared oversight of fiscal responsibilities, allocation of resources, and the acquisition of outside funding to support school-based initiatives. Obviously, some principals are more adept at this than others. Since a school's financial environment can be complex and unstable, research advises considerable training in budget-management practices and much time working through the school system's budgetary processes to achieve real efficiency in this area (Lawler, 1986, 1992, as cited in Wohlstetter & Mohrman, 1996).

Knowing the ins and outs of the district's budgetary system, a process that emanates from a centralized database, may present another hurdle. For example, when St. Louis city schools upgraded to a "more efficient" computerized program for tracking allocations and submitting requisitions, even with training, bugs in the system made for stressful times at site offices. A few principals, uncomfortable with the new budgetary package, delegated that responsibility. This may resolve your concerns about spending long hours at a computer, away from an instructional leadership role. However, as principal, you must retain budgetary accountability, be knowledgeable about your school's financial position, and be confident in the staff you've selected to handle fiscal responsibilities.

The knowledge base required for superior budgetary operations in the school is extensive. An in-depth examination of the specifics and the steps associated with the above budgetary and fiscal processes goes beyond the scope of the school-based practices treated here. A number of texts, however, cover the intricacies of selected budgetary approaches (e.g., Candoli et al., 1998; Thompson & Wood, 2001). For more information, helpful Internet sites present useful materials on budget planning and fiscal systems. Highly informative is the "Financial Accountability System Resource Guide" posted on the Web by the state of Texas (Texas Education Agency, 2002). Another useful resource is the on-line "Budget Builder Analysis." It discusses the development of the Budget Builder Web site. Budget Builder, a tool that explains and simplifies budgeting at the school level, is used by the Seattle public school district (Halaska, n.d.).

Schools of education in colleges and universities afford a range of courses in budget development, fiscal procedures, and resource management. Key players on your SBM team should complete such a course and transfer their budgetary knowledge to school staff members. They can develop and use on-site professional development activities that focus on planning and monitoring the school budget. It might be a good idea to devise a simulation workshop that trains staff in budgetary techniques and calculations. The simulation could also cover the interpersonal and behavioral issues associated with budgetary discussions, fiscal reporting, and a trait that is always essential to financial negotiations, compromise.

A NOTE ON STATISTICAL DATA

Needs assessments, school improvement plans, and site-based budgets are built on statistical data in order to make the most reliable decisions possible. However, statistics can sometimes be misleading, especially if misinterpreted or presented from a biased perspective. It's important, therefore, to realize that numbers derived from test-score data, random surveys, or comparison studies may not always be entirely accurate or representative. Program promoters may use statistics to lead potential purchasers of educational products into positive conclusions without the verifiable evidence required to make sound decisions. Your budget planning committee should remain on guard against dubious statistical claims that are short on integrity and may not be possible to replicate at your school.

The reliability and validity of data sources depends on the nature of the tests used, the objectivity of the sources employed, or the true representation of the study sample. In your school's needs assessment, for example, the wording of survey questions, the number of people contacted, and the response rate should influence the amount of trust you place in the results gleaned from the data. Perhaps the best advice to a SBM budget committee is to keep an open, critical mind. In the final analysis, data-driven decision making is important, but students are not numbers. Children and young adults will always present individual needs and demonstrate unique abilities beyond the collective data used for budgetary decisions.

PARTICIPANTS IN BUDGET PLANNING

In Lewis Carroll's whimsical creation of Wonderland, narrow perceptivity becomes laughable. The rigidity of the White and Red Queens in seeing only what they want to see comes to mind. The White Queen asks Alice, "What's one and one and one and one and one and one and one and one and one?" "I don't know," said Alice. "I lost count." "She can't do addition," the Red Queen interrupts. And so it went, on and on through a delirious set of peculiar questions leading nowhere. If this brings to mind a school administrative meeting where input was asked but seldom used, you're not alone in your recollection. Unfortunately, school planning meetings sometimes represent Wonderland, not reality.

When it comes to reviewing concerns about school finances, whether expressed by parents, citizens, or staff members, on-site decision makers should not summarily dismiss well-meant input.

Plans made without weighing all of the information available represent decisions made by closed minds. Site-based budgeting implies joint decision making openly arrived at and freely communicated. Collegiality and cohesion will surely be essential when it becomes necessary to meet unexpected academic needs. Predetermined steps must be available to jointly present, review, and implement budget revisions during the school year, especially if strategic adjustments are required to improve student outcomes. The participants in the budget planning process must be identified, trained, well-informed about financial issues and school objectives, and on call to act when conditions warrant fiscal intervention.

SBM Formats

The type of SBM system in place at your school will determine those who have control of the school's purse strings. For example, the National Education Association and the American Federation of Teachers advocate democratic schools. The democratic style of SBM promotes collegial, participatory decision making that involves all or most staff and stakeholders. Collectively, these individuals provide input into all essential matters that contribute to the betterment of the school. Various teams or ad-hoc committees under the SBM umbrella address school needs. In some cases, when successes are realized and sustained, predetermined tangible rewards are provided to both the school and individual teachers.

Apple and Beane (1995) assembled four narratives of democratic schools. These types of schools share a commitment to discovering useful ways to improve the participation of all those associated with the school experience. Teachers, parents, members of the community, and students work together to uplift the academic success of the school. A variety of case studies of schools that have gone through resource reallocation and site-based team building are available for investigation. These reports are worth reviewing because they give detailed insights into some of the steps that take place when using SBM strategies (e.g., Odden et al., 1999).

In addition to the democratic style of SBM, another format is principal-directed, where the principal orchestrates the site-based budgetary process. This usually means principal consultation with staff members and parents for their input. Final budgetary decisions and the resolution of school financial matters, however, remain in the hands of school-site administrators.

Still a third variant of SBM is the school council or committee, usually composed of representative parents, teachers, and community members who are elected to act as a governing board for the school site. A school council may have broad control of fiscal allocations and expenditures, or they may focus on discrete budget areas. The school principal may or may not be a leading participant in this group.

SBM Parental Connections

When considering the composition of the school council or SBM team, parents are extremely important. Differences between home and school expectations can put students at risk of academic failure. Parents need to be in tune with school practices and have faith in school policies in order to support their child's education. If parents and guardians are not made aware of what the school needs from them in the way of home support for the child's education, they cannot provide assistance in a meaningful way. Strong partnerships between the school and families are critical to high levels of student success. Parental participation on the SBM team and input in the school-based budgeting process, with appropriate training provided, may be the way to strengthen parental involvement in the school.

In many districts today, however, attracting and maintaining parental participation is no easy matter. At some school sites, inspiring parents to become involved on a continuing basis simply may not materialize, no matter how appealing your school's activities (buffets, children's performances, guest speakers). In these cases, school staff members will be more actively involved in budgetary matters than parents.

In the city of St. Louis, for example, efforts to bring parents on board are promoted in every school by a variety of programs. However, as a middle school principal remarked, "Parent participation remains troublesome. It's my content-area teachers and grade-level teams who regularly review budget matters. They use our funds for learning and teaching aides upon which there's agreement, . . . materials that will help our students move toward performance standards."

Rates of outside involvement in the school depend on its organizational structure, whether students walk to school from nearby neighborhoods or are bused long distances, and the degree to which the school performs outreach to the community. Citizen participation on SBM councils varies greatly too. St. Louis city schools, for example, operate 16 Community Education Centers (CECs) strategically placed throughout the city. At these schools, parents and neighborhood citizens have a larger on-site role. They are directly involved in extended-day and after-school programs and services for children and adults.

The principal of a St. Louis CEC middle school facilitates data-driven linkages between her day and evening staff. Student assessment materials are shared so that academic support and tutoring services remain focused on individual pupil needs. The middle school uses a seamless budget to help make the connections among multiple services more meaningful. "It allows us to look at everything as one program," the St. Louis principal says in *After School Issues*.

> "Collectively, we can look at the whole picture of services offered during day and extended day and decide how we want the program to look and how we want the experiences to be integrated." Unmistakably, the involvement and leadership of the principal is required to reach this level of information exchange and budget utilization (Hall, 2002).

From yet another perspective, when SBM budgetary processes are well implemented, teachers, parents, and involved citizens are more likely to become aware of the school's financial situation and spending limitations. Community awareness regarding finances, in turn, develops a more concrete understanding of the costs required for essentials needed to produce academic results in the school.

Interestingly, shared financial awareness may have an impact beyond improved teaching and learning at the site. When the St. Louis public schools pushed to pass a bond issue to air-condition its schools, important for the summer program that provides inquiry-based instruction to thousands of students and meets the "No Child Left Behind" standards, active SBM councils turned out in support. Through a concerted effort with strong central-office leadership, guided by the superintendent, the need was effectively communicated to the public. Many St. Louis schools have been air-conditioned. A bonus to effective school-based practices, then, is that a well-structured SBM team can exert influence in the community beyond the school neighborhood.

Fiscal Behavior

Teachers, parents, citizens, and in some cases students, are the people whose individualistic natures will contribute to your SBM team. These personalities and their interactions will naturally reflect all of the complexities in human behavior. When planning site-based budgets, it may be wise to look into the economic theories advanced by Princeton University psychology professor Daniel Kahneman. Kahneman won the 2002 Nobel Prize in economics for explaining peculiarities in human nature that affect financial decision making. Behavioral finance reveals the irrationality that sometimes controls our money management decisions.

People involved in investing funds are looking to produce gains, but they may not always make perfectly rational monetary decisions. Those on your school's site-based budget committee are looking for gains too, gains in student achievement. Human nature dictates that judgment under conditions of uncertainty may blur abilities to see the entire economic picture. Mistakes that individual investors seem to make may be likened to mistakes that site-based budget managers could make. Financial errors to consider include the possibility that budget planners are swayed by an unrealistic optimism about their school's educational programs. Overconfidence that our decisions will always succeed, a rosy view of our own abilities and predictions, can lead to serious difficulties.

Site-based budgeting problems, for instance, might surface through an inability to comprehend the school mission in its totality. Planners could have a narrow focus on segmented components of a program rather than key in on the full effect of their investment in the entire school improvement plan. School leaders, like investors in stocks, may not like to admit a loss in a particular educational program, clinging to it when the evidence shows that gains have not, and most likely will not, be realized. In this regard, the SBM team must maintain a realistic view of the school's educational as well as fiscal situation. Behavioral finance theories shouldn't be overlooked when site-based managers convene to make decisions about the allocation of school funds for academic improvements.

It's important, too, that when SBM or any model becomes a system's or a school's course of action, whether in instructional, budgetary, or other matters, that it's the school's own choice, adapted to its needs, and not an externally spawned answer to problems that are perceived to be coming from the outside. "That doesn't mean the system won't seek strategies that others have found successful; it will. But the one adopted will have to be customized to the unique situation of the system" (Hutchins, 1996, p. 192).

The unique situation in your school will relate to the needs of the students, staff, parents, and members of the community who come together to work toward the school mission of educational excellence. A necessary element for accomplishing the school mission is a leadership style that encourages unity of purpose and instructional coherence.

CHAPTER 2 SUMMARY

School financial planning is more than dollars and cents, appropriations and expenditures, or making do with what you have. It's vital to recognize that budgetary decision making doesn't mean just mathematical computations. Decisions must be based on an awareness of the actual needs of the school population. While strong skills in financial analysis are required in the budgetary process, decisions to improve achievement are more than conditioned responses. Your decisions should be based on an in-depth understanding of the whole school community. Your data must be drawn from reliable needs assessments. Academic and instructional weaknesses are recognized and analyzed, and creative solutions are designed and implemented using a practical school improvement plan.

If your school uses a high-involvement, site-based budgeting system, your SBM team will control staff recruitment, expenses for substitute teachers and utilities, selection of the source of services and supplies, and year-to-year carryover of unspent funds. However, a more likely system of on-site budgetary authority is limited to the ability to redirect discretionary funds. The discretionary funds can be supplemented by outside resources applied to interventions that best accomplish im-proved student achievement.

In-depth training to gain knowledge in budgetary processes and fis-cal behaviors is a prerequisite to performing school practices that get results. An understanding of financial issues shows why it is critical that the school budget be connected to the needs assessment and the school improvement plan. While improved student achievement de-pends on the alignment of needs, goals, and objectives, it is the wise ap-plication of resources that dramatically affects short-term results and long-term gains. In this respect, site-based budgeting should provide your school staff members with the advantage of placing funds where they will do the most good for student academic accomplishment.

The SBM system in place at your school will determine those who have control of the school's purse strings. Site-based budgeting may be democratic, principal-directed, or council-oriented. In any case, con-sensus and consistency in the school program are essential. To record and monitor program finances, your school may use one or a combina-tion of the basic budgetary approaches: (1) line-item budgeting, (2) per-formance budgeting, (3) program-planning budgeting, (4) zero-based budgeting, or (5) outcome budgeting. Whatever the approach, a well-monitored cash management policy is a must.

Sound financial planning at the school requires a principal's direct or shared responsibility for fiscal matters and resource allocation. The SBM financial plan should include methods to obtain assets from out-side the system that will support school-based initiatives. When SBM and site-based budgeting are selected as the operational model by a school, it should be the school's own choice, adjusted to its unique needs and not externally mandated. Finally, trying to implement SBM without provisions for adequate leadership training and cohesive staff support likely will result in little success.

CHAPTER 2 REFLECTION AND DISCUSSION

1. What are some of the variations in site-based budgeting? Which method do you think would be most appropriate to meet the current requirements in your school?

2. What's the purpose behind a school needs assessment and what's involved in designing one that's effective? How does the needs assessment relate to budgetary issues? Does your school conduct regular needs assessments, and how are they used?

3. What goes into an effective school improvement plan? How is the SIP developed at your school? How might SBM strategies and site-based budgeting enter into staff discussions about your SIP?

4. What is the budget planning cycle? Why is budgetary evaluation important?

5. What are some budgetary approaches or formats? Which format is currently used in your school? Which approach or combination of processes do you think is best suited to SBM?

6. Why is it essential to have a well-monitored cash management policy at the school site?

7. What are the different forms of staff and community participation in SBM schools? What participatory style is currently in place at your school? What are some fiscal behaviors that might sidetrack a site-based budgeting committee?

CHAPTER 3

Consultative Leadership, Budgeting for Instructional Coherence

Back when baby boomers were flooding America's schools, actor Jimmy Stewart played Lt. Col. Robert "Dutch" Holland in the film *Strategic Air Command* (1955). Dutch, a star third baseman for the St. Louis Cardinals, is called back to active duty when the Air Force needs bomber pilots. Besides the fun of seeing Stewart in a Redbirds uniform, the film projects a strong image of team solidarity. When individualistic World War II fighter pilots undertake Cold War bomber duty, they must learn a new rating system. Accountability is assigned to the entire crew, not just to the pilot. Similarly, assessing school-based management and its facilitative function, site-based budgeting, requires judgments based on the whole school team. Still, the pilot maintains mission coherence. Dutch, wearing his St. Louis ball cap while at the controls of a huge B-36, remains in charge. In SBM, the school mission is piloted by the principal.

School-based management places considerable leadership responsibility in the hands of principals. The SBM principal must be highly skilled in order to fulfill managerial, financial, and instructional roles. The following discussion is therefore directed primarily at principals, assistant principals, or school leaders aspiring to the principalship. However, the information in this chapter is also designed to be of use to the SBM leadership team, that is, council members, grade-level and subject-area team leaders, instructional coordinators, program facilitators, schoolwide Title 1 teachers, and others filling positions of leadership responsibility in the school.

School leaders need to allocate time toward achieving educational excellence with the same degree of care that is put into the school's budgetary planning. This means budgeting time as well as resources toward instructional coherence. Unquestionably, the school's greatest resource is a close-knit instructional team with the ability to communicate through mutual understanding of the school's mission and goals. This ability grows with familiarity and trust, founded on a shared educational philosophy and shared experiences that contribute to student successes. Developing and sustaining a strong, affirmative school culture is not easy. Each year principals tackle bigger workloads with daily schedules often consumed by noninstructional concerns. On nationwide surveys, more than 80% of principals say they have more new responsibilities and mandates than they can handle. Pile on accountability to meet state standards topped off by high-stakes testing to win accreditation, and the job becomes truly formidable.

How can principals contend with diverse obligations and still give full attention to teaching and learning? Efficient principals use time management practices to prioritize and delegate. But meeting the challenges of a bulging workload and simultaneously raising students' test scores may require something extra.

As an educator and evaluator in a large public school system, I have observed that "something extra" in certain schools. I'm speaking of the uncanny knack some principals have for instilling coherence. It comes in part from what I call a "consultative style." In down-to-earth terms, I see successful principals as open-minded listeners, pointed counselors, and extraordinary salespeople.

Research says principals work in hierarchical, transformational, or facilitative modes. You can lead by mandate, mold a shared mission, or build participatory decision making. Not surprisingly, results-oriented leadership calls for a combination of these strategies.

However, you can't be effective merely by adopting a "textbook" managerial style. A natural way of doing things in tune with personal practices and beliefs works best. With a consultative approach, the principal listens to all stakeholders and counsels divergent views toward a common purpose. As needs and successes are communicated, each audience is sold on a school mission designed to build a coherent instructional framework.

CONSENSUS-BUILDING COHERENCE

Consultative principals are architects of program coherence. They watch the school's instructional framework rise toward its goal, improved academic achievement. As they gather input and interpret data from many sources, they gauge instruction and align it with district and state standards.

Information assembled from classroom observations and the concerns of colleagues and parents, when analyzed, holds other benefits. If we know how, we can use our collected findings to turn work-a-day concerns into creative payoffs.

For example, I was observing in a middle school where the principal came up against staff resistance to district-mandated reforms. Instructional innovations had been advised for some schools to help them accomplish state standards. The principal's school, certainly not alone in the system, did not measure up on the state's high-stakes performance test. Low-performing schools, identified by district administrators and spotlighted by the local media, received extra funds. Monies were allocated for teacher training and instructional materials to implement "research-based" reform models.

Schools had the opportunity to select a model of their choice. They could pick from a list of alternatives such as Accelerated Schools, Different Ways of Knowing, Success for All, and others. Well-implemented models, especially those that emphasize high-order learning and critical thinking, are said to contribute to improved student achievement. Even so, seasoned but leery teachers expressed concerns. Could "packaged" instruction work? Could a model benefit teaching, help students learn, and improve their school's cumulative scores on the state performance test?

His ear always to the school grounds, the principal quickly formulated a workable response. Grade-level teacher teams were counseled to conduct action research. Teams were advised to investigate and select a model. After they reached agreement, they were asked to find the best fit for it in their school improvement plan. A possible impediment—the principal could have mandated the model of his choice and risked alienating staff—instead turned into staff ownership. In the long run, a particular model may not be as important as staff buy-in to a coherent, learner-centered program.

This principal continues to promote coherence with the model his staff members selected. As lead teacher, he tries to avoid adversarial positions. "Why bushwhack those whose support is essential?" he asks. Adept at collaborative planning, he productively shares responsibilities.

This has smoothed introduction of instructional innovations into class-rooms and eased implementation of a plan designed to improve scores on the state performance test. Moreover, sharing accountability lets staff better see schoolwide problems and the common need to find solutions. The principal's consultative system does not seem contrived, either. It nurtures research-validated knowledge and collegiality. He knows, as studies show, that teachers are more apt to learn from one another than from instructional supervisors.

Teachers become more receptive to formative and summative evaluations when, under consultative leadership, they have some say in decisions. Shaping consensus toward instructional coherence keeps staff on the same wavelength and stymies divisiveness. The result is more time to explore ways to improve academic achievement.

Keys to Coherence

Research shows that instructional coherence can contribute to improved student achievement. The principal occupies a pivotal position from which to advance program coherence. But what constitutes coherence? First, a common instructional framework guides curriculum, teaching, assessment, and learning. Set expectations for student learning are tied to specific teaching strategies and assessment materials. These factors are important in many of the instructional models adopted by St. Louis schools and in other school systems throughout the nation. St. Louis also designed and made available to all teachers diagnostic quizzes aligned with the state performance assessment. Moreover, St. Louis administrators advocated districtwide "action strategies" developed to meet accreditation standards.

What else leads to coherence? The principal ensures that the working conditions in the school support staff stability and implementation of the instructional framework. Many districts nationwide adhere to a site-based management plan that allows for greater on-site control. The principal, more than anyone, should know when adequate resources are assigned to instruction and applied to meaningful professional development. Responsible fiscal oversight sees that resources are not spread thinly among layers of overlapping programs, or if multiple programs are in place, they are complementary and supportive of the instructional framework.

Too many programs in a school may lessen their systematic connection. This can lead to disparate players at odds with one another. You regularly need to ask, "Are any programs adversely affecting our ability to implement a coherent instructional framework? What can we do to eliminate them or align them toward improved student achievement to meet state standards?"

Instructional models aside, it's likely that program coherence is one of the best ways to positively impact achievement. This was shown in a correlation of standardized test outcomes and indicators of coherence in Chicago elementary schools. The Chicago study "found a strong positive relationship between improving coherence and improved student achievement. Schools that improved their instructional program coherence between 1994 and 1997 demonstrated improved student test scores over the same period of time" (Newmann et al., 2001).

Chicago schools that demonstrated instructional coherence shared certain factors. With strong principal leadership, team leaders instituted common instructional frameworks supported by schoolwide technical resources, such as quality curriculum and assessment materials. Extensive collaboration among staff was advocated. All resources were focused on one or a few schoolwide improvements. These efforts were sustained for three years or longer. In contrast, low ranking schools, those that believed commitment alone was sufficient to improve test scores, spread resources across numerous programs, usually involving different staff. An effort was made, but coherence remained weak and test scores static.

Other research points to the importance of developing instructional coherence to reach state standards. The Council of the Great City Schools and Manpower Demonstration Research Corporation (2002) compared four urban school districts that realized academic achievement gains with districts that did not see similar improvement. Findings in their report, *Foundations for Success,* showed that a shared districtwide vision to improve teaching and learning, extensive professional development, data-driven decision-making, and districtwide consistency of instruction or instructional program coherence had a positive effect on student achievement.

In the St. Louis public schools, a qualitative in-house study looked for common instructional practices that may have affected consistent improvement on the state performance test. Elementary schools that met the state standard for two years consecutively on the state's grade-level, subject-area tests were compared alongside a sample of schools that did not achieve similar results. In this study of staff perceptions, principal leadership that promoted coherence and staff stability was deemed highly important. It's likely that consultative principals employ methods that keep schools on track, maintaining and upgrading a logical instructional framework.

Factors that most affected consistent improvement on the state assessment in St. Louis included a combination of the following:

- School leadership ensures classroom practices fit within a coherent focus.
- Collegial, grade-level teacher teams deliver a cohesive, standards-aligned curriculum.
- Achievement data guide instruction; high-order skills and critical thinking are taught.
- Professional development is based on teachers' and students' needs, with follow-up.
- Performance materials are scored with rubrics; students assess one another's work.
- Extended-day/after-school, "fun learning" activities incorporate state standards.

FACILITATING COHERENCE

The consultative principal applies a variety of sound business practices and human relations skills to school management. Principals are generally flexible as they handle diverse concerns and facilitate instructional improvements. Flexibility is essential for solving complex problems and managing worthwhile programs. But what's new about that?

What may be new is taking stock of your role from a consultative perspective. If you're consultative, you're adept at observation, analysis, decision making, and action (proactive, not reactive). To get things going and keep things working, you know what to look for and where to find it. You're flexible in putting into place the school improvement plan. Pitfalls attached to premature evaluation of important issues ("knee-jerk" reactions) are avoided. You know where assistance is most needed, and all staff members receive help to produce results. Ultimately, this furthers attainment of academic goals.

Unfortunately, I've evaluated some schools where principals lack flexibility. They seem lassoed to their desks by red tape, hard pressed to meet demands. This detracts from their facilitative capacity to improve instruction. Without firsthand, day-to-day information as to what occurs in classrooms, we can hardly perform consultatively. What's worse, with inflexibility we may lose sight of an essential facilitative skill, our sensitivity to others. Try ironing out school hassles with a curt "See my assistant for that" and see how far it gets you in nurturing staff collegiality.

Delegating oversight to assistant principals, instructional coordinators, or mentor teachers is appropriate. But if we manage excessively, we may overrely on our most proficient staff as frontline instructional leaders. When we sidetrack our own instructional facilitative skills, we're stuck in a rut. Our flexibility in gathering and interpreting observational data suffers. The process of continually rechecking, determining alternatives, predicting outcomes, and carrying out sound, data-driven plans is diminished when too many instructional leadership responsibilities are assigned to others.

Conversely, I know a busy middle school principal who refuses to relinquish her role as facilitator of the instructional program. When student behavior began taking up more and more of her time, she made staff aware of the critical need for their contributions. Under her direction, the administrative aide, school secretary, and surprisingly, a parent volunteer now share oversight of student discipline. They even complete selected paperwork for the central office. (Getting parent volunteers involved with student behavior issues can prove quite effective in maintaining a learner-centered school climate.)

While this principal knows managing student discipline is important, she believes high visibility motivates staff and students. It's the best way, too, she says, to guide implementation of the instructional model. Regularly reviewing lesson plans and monitoring instruction helps her see which classrooms require reaffirmation of innovative practices and more emphasis on proven strategies. Sometimes she models constructivist, inquiry-based lessons drawn from her school's instructional model. Her top priority: "Destination accreditation! Keep 'em rollin' toward performance standards."

This principal exercises flexibility in supervision. She mentors new teachers, teams with others, and learns from those as experienced as she. Sensitive to the learning styles of her instructional staff, she attacks problems that if left unobserved, without analysis, could mushroom into schoolwide time-wasters or contribute to poor student performance. Some principals spend inordinate amounts of energy fighting fires. Consultative principals douse problems while still smoldering.

As we facilitate effective instruction, another asset comes into play. This middle school principal is keenly able to make patterns out of separate parts. As she expresses it, "Ongoing reassessment of instruction and learning allows me to see the bigger picture." You need the "bigger picture" for understanding the intricacies of a school. You need all the pieces of the puzzle and the skills to put them together. Otherwise, how can you assemble diverse programs into a coherent framework?

Puzzle Solvers

A poorly performing school is a complex puzzle, its pieces haphazardly scattered. The principal shares a vision of how the completed puzzle should look. Teachers, students, parents, support staff, community volunteers, and businesspeople all set to work assembling sections of the whole puzzle. But teams are not isolated. The principal facilitates, helping all stay aligned as each group fashions their part before fitting the vision together. The principal shows off the completed puzzle, acknowledging everyone's contributions. Now each better understands their relationship to the other and how their efforts holistically contribute to program coherence and improved student achievement. Coherence is the puzzle, diverse groups and interests the pieces.

Among diverse school constituencies are families. Family-school connections constitute an essential piece of the puzzle. Parents and guardians of students must be welcomed into the school to get to know teachers and other staff and to begin to attach the school culture to the home culture. Then the school can become an integral part of the community. Indeed, the successful neighborhood school can emerge as the focal point for revitalizing community spirit.

In addition to home-school connections, research shows that successful implementation of instructional reform models in some cases results in improved program coherence and raises student achievement levels. However, in order to succeed, model strategies must be widely infused into instruction (75–90% staff buy-in) and aligned with district curriculum and state standards. Even when a model is effectively implemented, positive movement on standardized test scores may take three years or more. In this scenario, it's imperative that all stakeholders remain focused.

In schools that have effectively implemented instructional models, principals are puzzle solvers. To fit diverse school needs into place and improve focus on state objectives, they perform supervisory roles as flexible facilitators of instructional practices. As helpers and diagnosticians rather than directors and tellers, they know, when practicable, how to modify instructional model components to meet unique school requirements.

For example, among several St. Louis middle schools that simultaneously adopted the same instructional program, two evidenced a degree of positive movement in student achievement outcomes. However, district evaluators who observed instruction in these schools assigned ratings for model implementation that varied widely, one high, one low. Teachers who were observed in one school had successfully incorporated model concepts across the curriculum, even into physical education. Instruction in mathematics and science when observed at the other school, however, did not present strong use of the model. Nonetheless, closer examination found that both schools displayed elements of improved program coherence. While math and science teachers at one school did not consistently use the model, they effectively integrated state performance objectives and high-order learning into daily lessons, and they got results.

A well-implemented instructional model may serve as an effective vehicle to achieve coherence. Variations on a model theme or a school's own learner-centered program that meets diverse teacher and student preferences, that is, flexibility in facilitating coherence, can also assemble the puzzle. Whatever the case, it's imperative that effective strategies become institutionalized within your school to counter the loss of school district funds should they suddenly dry up and disappear. (See figure 3.1.)

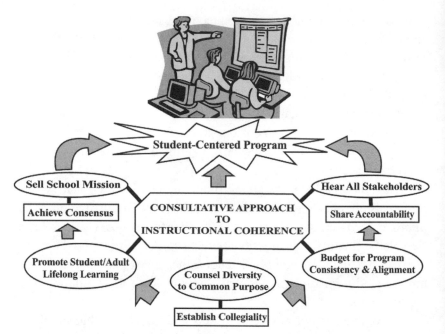

Figure 3.1.   A Consultative Approach to Instructional Coherence

LEADERSHIP MODELS

Along with instructional reform models, educators have applied a variety of formats drawn from the business world to school leadership and management. One of many business leadership concepts that has affected education is W. Edwards Deming's philosophy of Total Quality Management (TQM). TQM garnered wide circulation during the 1980s. By the late 1980s and into the 1990s, it had infiltrated educational circles. School systems launched initiatives to restructure education based on quality improvement. Often schools aligned reforms with the fourteen precepts of management and supervision, which Deming presented in *Out of the Crisis* (1986).

We'll not get into Deming's philosophy in detail, but some of the principles he advocates certainly apply to school-based practices in management, leadership, and fiscal control. A critical element advanced by Deming is the creation of "constancy of purpose" to improve product and service. Basically, this means that SBM leaders can't let the school program flop from one instructional fad to the next. We can't inflict worry about repeated change, quality, and costs that could have teachers saying, "And this too shall pass."

SBM leaders must stimulate innovation and improvement, but they must do so through the maintenance of consistent standards once the changes sought in school culture are instituted. And institutionalization of the instructional and learning program does not mean just paying lip service to the reforms. The new ideas must be fully accepted (in TQM lingo "adopted") by the large majority of school staff members. The reforms are made an integral part of the school's day-to-day life.

Another idea among Deming's fourteen principles centers on "total costs." In the business world, awarding contracts to the lowest bidders doesn't necessarily mean you'll be saving money over the long haul, especially when lasting quality and reliability of service are taken into account. An important part of total costs, often overlooked, is time. Time waiting for products to arrive and services to be performed is wasted time that adds to total costs. The SBM team can apply this precept to school financial planning and budgetary management. And, if they like, SBM leaders can take it a further step. How about your school's total costs when blocks of instructional time, for whatever reason, are lost because of student disengagement from the educational task?

TQM concepts address issues that affect virtually every dimension of SBM. These include institutional improvement, professional development, facilitative leadership, collaborative and mutually supportive teams, the removal of barriers that block the attainment of objectives, and other factors associated with getting results. Perhaps one of the most important of Deming's principles in terms of its application to school culture is "driving out fear."

Fear in the school environment inhibits creativity, risk taking, and innovation. Fear causes school staff members to operate defensively. When asked on nationwide surveys why talented teachers quit, more than 80% of superintendents and principals responded that it's because of politics and bureaucracy, elements that can stifle intellectual freedom.

Teachers policed by principals and principals, in turn, policed by central administrators create a system where instructional staff members are afraid of the consequences of their actions. They begin to say and do only that which is required to get by. This could lead to slanted perceptions. Biased reporting could perhaps begin to see the strengths in an educational program while overlooking the program's weaknesses. Convoluting the data into an inaccurate view of realities in the school serves no one. In this type of system, students suffer along with the staff, maybe more so.

Conversely, continuous improvement requires instructional leadership that drives out fear. Effective SBM leadership promotes openness, sharing, and freedom, tempered by accountability. Successful school leaders focus on trying, learning, and achieving, not on the possibility of failing or the avoidance of failure.

Many notions of leadership from the business and professional worlds can be associated with SBM strategies. For example, Kouzes and Posner (2002) examined the challenges of leadership. They identified five practices that are easily integrated into SBM techniques. These practices have application to the development of a consultative style directed at achieving instructional coherence. In this scenario, the effective leader challenges the process, inspires a shared vision, enables others, models the way, and encourages the heart.

The SBM principal and leadership team could easily adopt the above five practices. The leadership team is always looking for ways to improve and to learn. Moreover, school leaders positively communicate purpose and anticipate success. All school staff members are included in the planning process, with opportunities available to each for leadership development. The leadership team tackles difficult school tasks and shows by example the values that win success. Finally, the principal and the SBM team publicly support, recognize, and praise staff members for their accomplishments.

Bennis and Nanus (1985) point to traits of leadership that mesh with those outlined above. Foremost, perhaps, is that a true leader enables others to show initiative rather than constraining others by manipulation. In the effective SBM environment, the principal and the leadership team are so intent on achieving results that they compel others to follow. The SBM team defines and articulates the school mission, organizing meaning for the instructional staff. Teachers are drawn into positive action rather than coerced to perform tasks that may have little meaning in the classroom when staff members are left uninformed. In short, the SBM team understands the weaknesses and capitalizes on the strengths of the school. The team never surrenders to failure.

SCHOOL-BASED LEADERSHIP PRACTICES

In addition to the business-management research that supports SBM practices, extensive educational literature is devoted to coordinating and facilitating a school's improvement by providing leadership in teaching and learning. With guidance from the principal, the following discussion outlines several specifics that have application to the SBM leadership team.

Working closely with the SBM team, the principal involves all teachers in consultative communication, achieves staff consensus on the school mission and goals, and develops a schoolwide understanding of solving problems to meet the instructional needs of all students. In working with teachers for the attainment of educational excellence, the principal and the SBM leadership team provide guidance while they encourage participatory decision making. Among several roles and responsibilities, the principal and team members are helpful facilitators. They advance school achievement as they perform the following responsibilities:

- Advocate high expectations for staff and students.
- Instill curriculum-relevant, achievement-oriented methods and strategies.
- Promote a results-oriented, data-driven, purposeful school climate.
- Monitor instruction, learning, and classroom management toward improvement.
- Align classroom objectives and assessment with board goals and state standards.
- Control the budget and secure resources to support the academic program.

When direction is needed to improve classroom teaching methods and learning strategies, the principal and the SBM leadership team can provide appropriate observations and feedback to teachers as well as develop and deliver useful staff in-service training. When teacher participatory involvement is called for, the principal facilitates communication and promotes the interchange of teacher-initiated ideas (teacher teams, action research), sharing those strategies that have been proven effective by the school's instructional staff.

One primary function of the principal is giving clinical and systematic help to each teacher, taking into account individual teacher differences. The goal is to improve individual classroom instruction, student learning, and overall school performance. In this respect, the principal and the SBM leadership team function as an information conduit on teaching methods and learning strategies.

When appropriate occasions arise, the principal also helps communicate instructional objectives to students. The role of the SBM principal includes helping teams of teachers ensure that students achieve success in their learning and that students accomplish the outcomes that are sought from their schooling. The school instructional staff and the students benefit when the principal is both an instructional leader and a learning leader (DuFour, 2002). The principal guides instruction but also encourages teacher teams to focus on student mastery of skills and to identify and help individual students meet the educational standards. The principal promotes staff professional growth while sustaining a student-centered program conducive to learning.

The attainments of both students and adults in the school community are enhanced when the principal and SBM leaders model the importance of lifelong learning. The school can lead the entire community toward the acquisition of useful knowledge. Daily activities are incorporated into the routines of the principal and the SBM leadership team that ensure direct contact and communication with students and parents to promote the importance of learning beyond the schoolhouse walls.

Fundamental leadership practices for facilitating good instruction and high-involvement learning have been identified in the research. Some useful SBM leadership practices are outlined in table 3.1.

The principal and the SBM leaders in the school know that no single method or strategy will meet the needs of all teachers and students. The team draws on a wide range of teaching methods and learning strategies to assist teachers in meeting the needs of all students. Team members adapt useful methods and strategies to each teacher for maximum utilization and effectiveness. Instructional leaders understand the complementary nature of teaching and learning models and can integrate effective points from the models into classroom instruction. Equally important, the SBM team can translate the assessment of school needs and resources into a focused budget and well-conceived, student-centered operational plan.

Table 3.1.   Some SBM Leadership Practices

Sell School Mission	Facilitate Learning Program	Create Positive Climate
• Help determine where to focus attention and resources • Define performance goals in measurable terms • Coordinate manageable, attainable objectives • Review goals periodically with teachers, students, parents, community members • Establish partnerships and resource linkages with community organizations and businesses	• Observe classroom instruction on a regular basis • Provide written feedback to teachers for improving teaching and learning • Help align curricular objectives with course content, state standards, and achievement tests • Establish continuity and coherence in curriculum across grade levels • Understand standardized and criterion-referenced testing • Interpret and use test results and other data to assess curriculum, instruction, and student progress	• Foster practices to limit interruptions to classroom learning time • Deliver in-service training activities to improve instruction and learning • Interact with teachers and students to informally promote school priorities • Encourage mastery of defined student skills, set high expectations for all • Recognize and reward effective teachers, share their methods/strategies • Praise students for academic achievement and improvement

The actions in the following list suggest specific activities that the SBM leadership team might take to improve teaching effectiveness and learning outcomes.

- Encourage the pursuit of a challenging academic mission in a safe, secure environment.
- Help teachers set and reach standards aligned with state and "No Child Left Behind" goals.
- Implement ongoing systems for recognition of academic success.
- Advocate the use of appropriate classroom measurements for student academic performance.
- Help encourage attendance, maintain classroom decorum, and engage students.
- Ensure that curriculum scope and sequence exist and are adhered to in classroom instruction.
- Show some knowledge and interest in each curriculum.
- Help acquire and supply resources and materials to complete staff instructional tasks.

- Listen actively to faculty ideas and create opportunities for teachers to express ideas.
- Support appropriate teacher decisions and needs with action.
- Provide opportunities for collaborative teacher planning, teaming, and action research.
- Analyze and share student assessments with teachers to address instruction and learning needs.
- Provide demonstration lessons infusing effective innovations into classroom teaching.
- Plan, conduct, and assess teacher in-service training.
- Make sure each teacher's instruction receives written formative and summative assessment.
- Provide direct instructional assistance in one-on-one interactions with individual teachers.
- Access support programs with input from staff on school and student needs.
- Help establish direct contact between parents and teachers.

Current research suggests that collaborative decision making among school staff members guided by facilitative instructional leadership contributes to a coherent school mission. This helps to build consensus for academic improvement. In this educational environment of whole-school reform, staff relationships are developed and maintained around shared instructional principles and professional values rather than bureaucratic roles. In large measure, it's the principal and SBM team who establish this school culture of achievement-based, results-oriented leadership. Consultative leadership is a style that will prove beneficial, too, as you search for and acquire the resources that will sustain and uplift your school's academic program.

BREAKING THROUGH TO CONSULTATIVE LEADERSHIP

"Breaking through" is an age-old philosophical concept probably easier to sense than to define. Breaking through occurs when you grasp the significance and interconnectedness of the whole. We are all tied to one reality much bigger than ourselves. You may have experienced times of breaking through, perhaps growing out of some tragedy in life, without really being able to describe the higher consciousness you had achieved. Applied to an educational setting, a breakthrough might be grasping the "big picture" in your school as you develop consultative leadership and move toward instructional coherence.

A generation ago and longer, a small circle of introspective thinkers who passed through Monterey, CA, considered and wrote about breaking through. Four scholarly minds shared thoughts on how the human condition could break through personal barriers and biases to a fuller realization of humanity's inherent possibilities. You may recognize the four: marine biologist Edward Ricketts, novelist John Steinbeck, poet Robinson Jeffers, and mythologist-philosopher Joseph Campbell.

Ricketts in 1939–40 penned thoughts on breaking through. He recalled an encounter as a child that joined him to another's hurting and created in him a strong need for giving. "There could be no expression adequate to that glowing feeling of kinship with all things and all people," wrote Ricketts. Steinbeck touched on breaking through in stories and novels. He immortalized his friend, Ed Ricketts, as the character Doc in *Cannery Row* (1945) and *Sweet Thursday* (1954): "Doc would listen to any kind of nonsense and change it for you to a kind of wisdom. His mind had no horizon—and his sympathy had no warp."

Earlier, Jeffers had captured the essence of the concept and used the phrase "break through" in the narrative poem "Roan Stallion" (1925): "Humanity is the mold to break away from, the crust to break through, the coal to break into fire." And Campbell knew that we have experiences all the time that give us an inkling of where our "bliss" is; it's up to us to "grab it." In the PBS documentary *The Power of Myth* (1988), Campbell said, "You have to learn to recognize your own depth. All the time. It is miraculous."

Breaking through is an awakening usually triggered by some shared experience. No predetermined set of events causes it; it just happens. The event is symbolic of the difficulties we all confront, commonalities that bind us as we seek answers and meaning to life's endeavors. For example, picture a principal and a teacher team engaged in a highly heated discussion. Their debate examines the challenges and rewards of full inclusion in the classroom. The principal, who has always favored student tracking, listens intently. Invited to observe and take part in teaching a full-inclusion class, the principal, interacting successfully with the children, suddenly "awakens" to a broadened perspective of cooperative learning, individualized education, multiple intelligences, and the latent potential awaiting discovery in each child. The principal has broken through to a higher plane of understanding. And this new understanding of teaching and learning is retained in day-to-day efforts to accomplish the school mission.

CHAPTER 3 SUMMARY

Research says principals spend more time than they would like dealing with issues other than teaching and learning. And each year principals acquire more noninstructional responsibilities. As a result, classroom observations, staff development, and student academic needs may suffer. Excessive time spent on handling managerial chores can hamper efforts to establish a coherent instructional framework.

The principal and the SBM leadership team can take practical steps to provide greater focus on instructional program coherence. The entire school community reaps rewards when the principal advances program coherence and serves as both an instructional leader and a leader of learning. Students, parents, teachers, and community members benefit when the principal and SBM leaders model the importance of lifelong learning. In this school setting, the entire community profits from the coherent instructional program.

An extensive literature on leadership exists in business and in education. Complementary concepts can be drawn from both fields that contribute to a definition of what constitutes effective school-based practices. As a first step, school improvement requires leadership that eliminates fear. Effective SBM leadership focuses on openness, sharing, and freedom, tempered by accountability.

Successful school leaders improve academic outcomes not by finding excuses for failure but by trying, learning from mistakes, and never accepting failure as an option. At the forefront of the SBM leadership team, the principal brings all teachers into consultative communication, achieves consensus on the school mission, and builds a schoolwide understanding that finds solutions to meet the instructional needs of all students.

Consultative leadership may be the formula that puts you and your school on the path to successfully meeting expanded responsibilities. The principal and the SBM team together can develop a consensus-building, facilitative leadership style. A combination of savvy in hearing the concerns of others, thoughtful input to solve problems, and emphasis on selling the school mission can enhance school-based practices that get results. Whether you've adopted a nationwide reform model or use a sound, locally developed program, consultative leadership may help you bolster instructional coherence, improve student achievement, and more readily meet state standards.

CHAPTER 3 REFLECTION AND DISCUSSION

1. How do you define "consultative leadership"? Why is the role of the principal so critical to this style of leadership and to the effectiveness of SBM?

2. What are the key elements that account for instructional coherence? Has coherence been established in your school? How?

3. To what extent can the principal delegate oversight for instructional leadership responsibilities to other SBM leaders in the school? What is the "big picture" in a school, and how do you get it?

4. What does it mean for the principal to be an instructional leader and a learning leader?

5. How does "constancy of purpose," one of the TQM principles, fit into the SBM leadership framework? What other concepts from TQM could be applied to school leadership that achieves instructional coherence?

6. How might "fear" affect the organizational structure of a school system?

7. What are some specific SBM leadership activities that should be observable in a well-functioning school? Do you see these activities practiced in your school? How do these practices affect school culture?

CHAPTER 4

Acquiring the Resources for Academic Success

The American hero who opened the airways of the world to transcontinental travel encountered turbulence on his flight path to obtain the resources he needed. Nonetheless, Charles A. Lindbergh persevered, found financial backers, and changed history. In his *Autobiography of Values* (1992), Lindbergh wrote, "Weeks of planning and frustrating effort passed, during which I had obtained only a single pledge." Hard work eventually paid off when eight St. Louis businessmen came to Lindbergh's rescue and funded his proposal. Then, with more than enough money to meet his needs, Lindbergh remarked, "To my amazement, I found buying the plane as difficult as it had been to get my project financed" (pp. 71–72).

In the film *The Spirit of St. Louis* (1957), actor Jimmy Stewart (perhaps a little old for the role) portrays the lanky pilot who completed the first nonstop, transatlantic flight from New York to Paris. As we become involved in the movie, we identify and empathize with Lindbergh, aloft and alone. The tenacious aviator struggles to stay awake and remain alert, fighting to reach his goal.

School staff members who take on the challenge of raising funds to get worthwhile educational projects off the ground must follow a flight plan and stay on course. In flush times, acquiring financial support for your school programs is not a simple task. When state and federal funds for public education become less plentiful, searching for and securing needed resources gets more frustrating. Like Lindbergh, when the monies are found, implementing the project to achieve your goal—sustained academic improvement—may be as difficult as it had been to get your project financed, maybe more so. That's the time to recall Lucky Lindy. "Stick-to-it-ive" people get results.

In recent decades, many educators have expected that tax revenues would provide the bulk of necessities believed to comprise good schooling. However, a look into the past shows that America's schools, especially those in rural areas with relatively greater operational costs for small, isolated sites, have always relied on outside sources to raise funds.

In regions where economic downturns and unremitting poverty affect tax bases, where industry is leaving and population declining, or where growing numbers of fixed-income senior citizens cannot bear an increased tax burden, the expectation that tax revenues alone will fund adequate schools may be unrealistic. Supplemental fundraising to enhance school activities is no longer a luxury. In many school districts, seeking resources from outside the system has become a necessity in order to maintain essential school programs and services.

The first step in acquiring money from sources outside your school is to assess the actual situation in the instructional and learning program inside your school. Then formulate a well-conceived plan of attack and a budget that will rectify the lack of essentials needed for academic growth. Proposals for requested funds should be tied to specific, identified student needs. If you've done your homework on the school's needs assessment, improvement plan, and budget, proposals for outside funding shouldn't be time consuming. In a SBM system, creating and managing a schoolwide or targeted program budget should not take any more time, and maybe less, than is required in a centralized system that demands numerous approvals, sign-offs, and the shuffling of layers of official forms.

Once the working budget for the innovation is together and on paper, it's time to begin looking for your sources of money. Align your projects with your funding sources. Don't copy school-district personnel who go on fishing expeditions. They'll apply for any monies they can lay their hands on, without fully comprehending how those funds, often earmarked for specific, delineated applications, will address the most pressing academic needs of their students.

Given the above circumstances, understanding key financing issues in education is essential. The school leadership team must acquire knowledge of the importance of school finance and comprehend the interrelated functions of budgeting, purchasing, payroll, human resource management, and financial reporting within the structure of the school system and within the framework of the general public. The team needs to be on top of the costs of all on-site programs as well as the trends in available funding sources. This requires ongoing research into grant-making institutions. The SBM budget planners, especially, must be able to answer questions about how the overall school program, or a targeted initiative, can acquire the specific fiscal resources it needs.

When it comes to discovering the monies you need, a big factor is not to be shy. Asking for resources is not always an agreeable task. As with any skill, you have to learn how to do it. A firm conviction that your efforts are not akin to panhandling helps. Always be aware that you're securing funds for what is one of the most important functions in your community, effectively educating its youth. Quality instruction and learning require adequate resources. When public financing of a school's needs are less than adequate, it's up to a dedicated SBM team to find ways to make up the shortfall.

One of the most effective methods in asking for assistance is to approach the selected prospect with a concise, honest, and enthusiastic request. Research into fundraising strategies shows that the reason most people say they give is simply that they are asked by someone they know. Other reasons include being a volunteer in the organization and being motivated to assist by hearing or reading a news story. Businesses cite public image and responsibility to the community as two important reasons for giving.

Financial resources that are available to the school will be accessed through several levels of opportunity. Local money-making events to underwrite short-term needs do not fall within the same purview as going after long-term developmental funds or designing grant proposals for big-ticket projects. Different strategies are required for the successful acquisition of resources that are sought within the various funding arenas.

Managing and keeping sustainable funds requires a combination of diverse strategies that draw upon multiple resources. A successful funding plan attacks the challenge of meeting school needs from all possible viewpoints and does not unduly rely on any single strategy. A comprehensive network of funding sources, a mix of small and large donors who give on a steady basis, should be your target. Your funding strategies should follow the adage: "Don't put all your eggs into one basket." (See figure 4.1.)

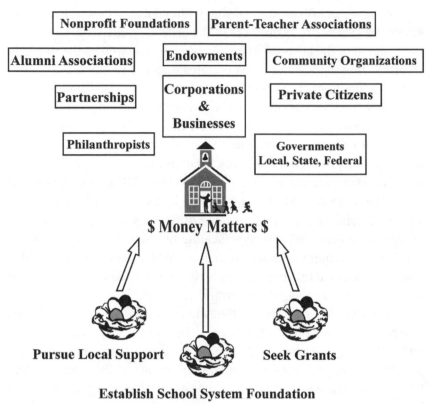

Figure 4.1.   Fundraising Opportunities

DOWN-HOME FUNDRAISING

It's likely that at one time or another most schools have tried some type of fundraiser to finance a particular school need. Examples include activities to cover the costs of band uniforms, athletic equipment, or travel expenses for the debating team. School-centered funding options cover a wide range of on-site events. These efforts can bring volunteer support into the school as well as raise some of the monies needed for educational programs. And the funds you can accumulate through local efforts add up to more than small change. Schools and nonprofit groups raise about $2 billion annually with local fundraisers.

The conditions in the neighborhood that surrounds your school and the larger socioeconomic makeup of your district play a role in determining what methods will be used to raise funds locally. The financial circumstances of families and businesses in the community that the school serves must be taken into account.

Fundraisers should not consistently draw upon the same supporters. Families and concerned citizens can do only so much. Before long, repeating your message to the same audience will begin to sound like static. If your activities to secure funds become annoying, your campaigns will be switched off. And a message ignored is an opportunity lost.

Plan fundraising events among district schools so as not to alienate your base of support. Some families have children at all school levels, and donating to each at the same time may be burdensome. It's important, too, to know what the potential competition is for money in your community. If an adjacent school system or nearby private and parochial schools are conducting fundraising campaigns, it would be wise to schedule your efforts so as not to coincide with theirs. However, schools in the same district can sometimes cosponsor an event and share in the promotional costs and the proceeds.

Among the tried-and-true money makers at the local level are parent bake sales, student club car washes, and raffles or auctions of items donated by community supporters. Schools can accumulate money for worthy projects through a number of fundraising happenings. Ideas run the gamut from benefit concerts to school-sponsored dances and plays to donation cans at local supermarkets. Many schools have set up recycling collection stations sponsored by local recycling companies. Parents and neighbors deposit paper or any number of recyclable items at the station located on the school grounds, and funds go to the school.

You might solicit funding ideas from local service organizations representing chapters of the Lions Club, the Kiwanis Club, or the Rotary International. Literally hundreds of Internet sites provide ideas and contacts to develop school fundraising plans. Catalogs and newsletters are widely available on fundraising topics, with tips for success. There is no telling where a terrific funding concept may turn up.

Monies raised by the above means can be supplemented with candy or cookie sales, a more traditional route to pulling funds into the school. Make sure companies are reputable and products are of high quality. Make doubly certain that mechanisms are in place to assure that the school sales teams maintain an orderly delivery of products and that the flow of money into the school's accounts is carefully checked and regulated. Be aware that many schools, for reasons of child safety, no longer allow their students to make door-to-door sales. If door-to-door sales are your best option, expect that an adult will be close by to monitor the student salesperson.

In many school systems today, parent–teacher associations (PTAs) take on some of the responsibilities of raising money. PTAs raise funds to supplement all variety of student activities that organization members see as important. Sometimes PTAs will provide a monetary award for each classroom teacher in the school to purchase learning materials for students. If you're fortunate enough to have an active PTA in your school, it's possible that its members may not consider fundraising a major item on their agenda. Regardless, their support is essential to implement SBM fundraising plans.

In all cases, your funding ideas must be well-publicized so that your school moves beyond the break-even point and makes a tidy profit. Don't forget to talk to the local media to see if newspaper space or radio and TV spots can be donated to disseminate word of your fundraiser. Or go a step farther and develop a media strategy like that of the schools in Richmond, VA, and other districts across the nation—raise money with a locally broadcast telethon.

An essential point to local fundraising activities is that you educate your community about the need that your school faces. Have a clear plan for your project and communicate the steps that you'll take to accomplish it and the standards on which you'll be evaluated. Many members of the community are willing to help when they know the details of your educational cause and understand your school's objectives to reach higher academic standards.

Education reformers have stressed the importance of a general series of steps schools can take to win community support (Solomon & Ferguson, 1998). When designing a fundraising campaign, it may be smart to keep these measures in mind. Basically, the procedures encompass establishing a vision for improvement, showing the need for change, bringing together representatives of all stakeholders in a leadership team, adjusting strategies for consistency, sharing information with all parties, selecting a workable model, and evaluating and reporting on progress.

SCHOOL-SYSTEM FOUNDATIONS

A growing number of school systems are establishing their own local education foundations to support their fiscal needs. The local education foundation (LEF) spearheads fundraising efforts for the schools in the system that it represents. When establishing a LEF, it's best if its tax status is that of a nonprofit 501(c)(3) organization. This allows corporations, foundations, and philanthropic donors of large sums to use tax deductions and other financial incentives when making contributions.

When donors have the opportunity to shelter a substantial portion of their charitable gifts to schools, they are more easily persuaded to participate in community initiatives to improve public education. Under the LEF format, donors may exercise options when contributing to the schools. They can donate to an annual, general fundraiser or, if they prefer, earmark their contributions for specific projects and programs.

Indeed, without a LEF, limitations are placed on the number of grants for which a school system may apply. While the school district may go after state and federal government grants, its LEF will likely be eligible to apply for three times as many grants as the district can access. This is because a much larger number of education grants are available from private foundations, especially during economic periods when public funding is evaporating. If your school system operates under per-pupil limitations on expenditures, foundation monies could possibly be used to bypass restrictions prescribed by local spending caps.

LEF boards are generally composed of community leaders and businesspeople, first-rate volunteers who have the best interests of the schools at heart. The bylaws of the LEF will establish what proportion of donations will be retained in a systemwide endowment and what proportion will be funneled directly into the schools. For example, near Boulder, CO, the St. Vrain Valley School District covers more than 400 square miles, serves more than 20,000 students, and encompasses a dozen communities. The St. Vrain LEF invests half of the contributions it receives in an endowment that makes its foundation self-perpetuating. Remaining funds are made available for school and program disbursement. In a districtwide LEF, individual schools and teachers can submit their proposals to the district's foundation for mini-grants or innovation grants.

Amounts raised by a LEF can be substantial. In St. Louis, MO, the public school system has garnered millions of dollars in support from corporations, private foundations, and national funding organizations. These are monies raised beyond state and federal government funding. Through grants to the St. Louis city schools, which serve more than 40,000 students, various funds flow into individual school programs, districtwide initiatives in science and mathematics, and professional development activities focused on school leadership and closing the achievement gap.

Small school districts that generally would not have a chance at large private grants should consider creating foundation cooperatives. One foundation can be established to serve the interests of a number of small districts.

For example, more than a dozen New Jersey school districts are represented by the countywide Cape Educational Technology Alliance (CETA). Each of the CETA school systems enrolls 2,500 or fewer students, and they work jointly in accessing funding packages. Granting sources look for broad impact when they disperse funds, and there is strength in numbers when applying for support. While the thrust of CETA is oriented toward technology, new ideas in other instructional and curriculum areas have been shared among the cooperating school districts.

Similarly, in Indiana, a cooperative foundation was awarded almost $5 million from the Lilly Endowment, Inc., under that endowment's Community Alliances to Promote Education (CAPE) program. Among several Lilly grantees who applied for CAPE funds, recipients in the Hancock County Community Foundation represented a collective that included four county school systems, the county community college, and the county library. The foundation successfully defined the educational needs of its community and presented a plan of proposed solutions. Several educational institutions are now sharing the funds from the grant.

While the Hancock County Community Foundation was not among the original CAPE grant recipients, foundation advocates persisted (remember Lucky Lindy). Under a grant extension, Hancock resubmitted a revised proposal and won its needed funds. Patience is an attribute in securing outside funding for school programs. After you've completed the extensive research, planning, and proposal writing required by the granting agency, it may take an additional year of revising, negotiating, and developing a relationship with the grantors before you see the requested funds to carry out your program.

If your school system does not have a local education foundation, it should seriously consider approaching a financial advisor, an accountant, and your district's attorney to establish one. Often, community professionals who have the expertise to set up a LEF will volunteer their time to the schools that serve their children.

As with any project, before looking into the establishment of a LEF it's best to develop a sound familiarity with the subject. Review the literature. Considerable material, published and on the Internet, identifies and describes grantors such as the Bill and Melinda Gates Foundation, the Lilly Endowment, or the Wallace–Reader's Digest Funds. Numerous sources outline the requirements of selected foundations and provide tips for making applications for funds. Almost every major educational association and organization has information available on setting up a LEF and securing resources for your school.

For example, like several educational publications, an entire issue of *Principal Leadership* magazine (January 2003) explored the topic of raising and managing funds for schools. Published by the National Association of Secondary School Principals, the thematic issue discussed ways for school leaders to start going after billions of dollars that private schools and universities have cashed in on for decades (Levenson, 2003).

Educators and professional fundraisers are in agreement that we have crossed a threshold. Public schools must approach foundations, corporations, government agencies, citizens, and alumni for funding assistance geared toward school reform and the improvement of academic outcomes.

GRANT SEEKING

With or without the aid of a LEF, your school can go after funding from government and small corporate and business sources in your area. Basically, there are two competitive grant-seeking approaches to pursue. A request for proposals (RFP) is based on established purposes and award criteria set by the funding source. These grants involve preset requirements, guidelines, and a timeline that must be adhered to. Another approach is to proactively search out funding sources from among private organizations and foundations. Many sources have funds available to assist worthwhile community education projects.

With the approval and support of your school principal and district superintendent, you can actively search your city, region, and state for appropriate grants. To do so and be successful requires solid skills in finding the correct sources, designing workable proposals, and writing effective grant applications.

There are a couple of things to be aware of before beginning your grant-seeking endeavors. Securing funds usually takes a lot of time and hard work. Sometimes a great idea presented in a well-written proposal and submitted to the right prospect will be rejected. But you can always submit the proposal to other groups, provided you change the format to meet the new criteria. More than 90% of grant proposals are turned away, but usually because the request was submitted to the wrong source or the application procedures were not correctly followed.

With the above factors in mind, it's up to you to find the local corporations, businesses, and public entities that are regularly looking for suitable community projects to support. Businesses and philanthropists have the monies to donate to help their hometowns, but they don't always have the ideas and the worthwhile programs that will address community needs with workable solutions. That's where your SBM leadership team comes onto the stage. The SBM team brings the school and its community into dynamic collaboration with local benefactors. To do so requires that you follow step-by-step procedures in your search for funding dollars.

There is much preparation to do before you write your grant proposal and complete a formal application for funding. Professional grant seekers generally say that three-fourths of the work required to procure a grant occurs before the writing of the proposal.

The first step, obviously, is to establish the need that exists in your school. What is it that requires fixing that will have a positive impact on student academic success? Examine your school needs assessment, improvement plan, and budget. These documents should provide helpful data to support your grant request.

Once you've defined your need, the next step in the grant preparation process includes researching and analyzing funding sources and reviewing their guidelines in order to select the best possible source. Finding the right granting source is critical. The prospective grantor must be a good fit with your project objectives. If a granting agency or corporation is interested in expanding the useful application of technology to solve local problems, don't submit a proposal that lacks technology infusion. If the rules for receiving a grant require your school or district to provide matching dollar amounts, and many grants do, make sure that you have the money to make the money.

Write your proposal only when you know as much as you can about the source to which you will submit it. This may mean contacting donors and conducting preliminary discussions about the project you have in mind. You may end up refining your concept to encompass particular concerns that the granting source thinks are important.

When the above procedures have been completed, write, edit, and proofread your grant proposal. Readability is a must. Keep to the point and avoid educational jargon. Have every member of the SBM team read and review all grant instructions and the finished written product. Discuss the instructions as a team to be sure that your completed proposal is in compliance with all grant stipulations. If instructions state that specific topic areas should be addressed in the application, make sure you cover all of them. Failure to follow grant instructions, disregarding important points, or missing the grant deadline for submission of your application will usually result in a denial of your request.

After you've submitted the proposal, there may be a series of questions and answers, follow-up activities, requested modifications, and contract negotiations to complete before you receive your funds. With your funds in hand, implement your program, evaluate and report on it to the grantor, and reassess your needs for continuing funding support.

Depending on the size of your school system, and whether it has a LEF, efforts to secure large funds may benefit from experienced grant writers as consultants. However, a teacher/administrator team, composed of those who know the nuts and bolts of the system and are well trained in grant writing procedures, should take the lead in planning and preparing fundraising activities. The SBM leadership team at the school site benefits, too, when they complete up-to-date courses or workshops in fundraising and grant-writing practices.

Basic formats and templates for preparing grant proposals are available in published materials and on the Internet. There is no single best way to put together your proposal. Generally, however, the grant proposal will include seven essentials. These are: (1) a cover letter and title page; (2) an executive summary; (3) the statement of need; (4) a description of the project with measurable goals, objectives, and a timeline; (5) an itemized budget (don't pad it) with brief explanations for dollar amounts assigned; (6) pertinent information on the school or district; and (7) a conclusion that reiterates the main points of the proposal.

Be sure that you build a realistic evaluation plan into the project description and know who the evaluators will be. All participants in the funded program will want to see an objective appraisal of its implementation, outcomes, and cost effectiveness. If professional development is necessary for effective implementation to occur, don't skimp on training costs in your proposal budget.

FISCAL DECISION MAKING

Finding resources will require maintaining a balance among diverse, sometimes conflicting, interests within your school and district. Compromise is an essential ingredient in winning meaningful resources. Remember that strings will usually be attached to decisions about where the money comes from and how and by whom it will be spent.

For example, similar to most urban school systems, in the city of St. Louis there are limits on the extent of fiscal control and decision-making responsibilities delegated to the schools. In any district, the central administration's SBM guidelines (and behind-the-scenes turf wars or power plays within the school) can restrain a free hand in finding and allocating resources. If a newly elected board of education takes the helm bent on quick "reform," as occurred in St. Louis in 2003, your SBM team may face the compound challenge of working under contracted corporate management while adjusting to deep fiscal cuts and staff reductions.

It's hard work to take advantage of on-site opportunities that may lead to the placement of useful assets in schools. It's even harder in a dysfunctional SBM environment, where the principal and leadership team may be unwilling (perhaps justifiably so) to collaborate fully with instructional staff on matters of school finance. However, as a St. Louis SBM facilitator once told me, "Principals *cannot* enter into combat with teachers. . . . Staff must be aligned. All must work together to rectify their school's shortcomings."

Dynamic leadership provided by a group of key people with determination to secure needed resources is important for effective fiscal decision making to take hold. Often school programs are sustained by creative thinkers who know how to look for support within and outside their communities. To retain and fine-tune proven academic programs and keep them going over the long term, key leaders on the SBM team must be able to locate sustainable funding.

Keeping school programs alive takes a variety of resources and the creation of a diverse funding portfolio. You should expect to garner assistance from federal, state, local, and private sources. Moreover, the entrepreneurial team that puts together diversified funding packages will help school programs remain stable. With a variety of resource providers, program leaders will not have to scramble to replace funds when an entire grant disappears. This degree of maintaining and replacing numerous resources, that is, sustaining multiple supports, requires deep collaboration on the part of the SBM team.

Divisiveness is always a concern when the merits of programs and services come up for discussion. Unfortunately, in a static or negative school climate, establishing funding priorities among programs may deteriorate into issues of a personal nature.

A trusting school climate appears to be a significant prerequisite to bringing outside resources into the school. Implementing school-based practices requires a close relationship among staff built on trust. SBM principals who acknowledge and reward effective teachers can capitalize on the staff's intrinsic motivation. With recognition and encouragement, teacher teams are more likely to use their capabilities to accomplish school instructional objectives. They are also more willing to heighten their visibility in the community in the search for needed resources.

For example, a recent survey of St. Louis public schools found that 80% of the staff at an area high school supported the school's instructional program as appropriate to the needs of its students. The principal and administrative team, who practice SBM strategies, attract a variety of outside resources, and they know that resources can be more than dollars and equipment. The school established its own link with a high-profile computer manufacturer to acquire a wireless, traveling computer lab; the portable set-up enhances students' research with Internet access from classroom to classroom. The principal and administrative team at this school crafted a partnership with a large insurance company, and the firm's workers provide after-school tutoring to students in the school.

In a well-functioning SBM environment, the school community begins to think collectively. Cost-effectiveness strategies come into play. Councils, usually under guidance from the principal, engage in regular dialogue: "Within parameters set by our state's and district's standards, let's examine useful teaching methods and lesson materials. What programs work and which can we *afford*? What stays, what goes?"

When everyone is more accountable at the school, the school management team tends to spend money more carefully. If your situation is such that you can carry over unspent funds, you can plan and use resources more efficiently. Setting aside funds for future, well-planned use is surely preferable to spending all remaining monies quickly at the end of the school year on whatever comes to mind, knowing the funds will be lost if not used.

Exercising selectivity among program choices also protects valuable resources. Funds are not diluted among disjointed efforts that may lack systematic connection. Ideally, a coherent instructional framework receives top priority. This is difficult in the face of pet projects among school staff or, especially, if the central office mandates particular programs that must be implemented, regardless.

But the central office, let's remember, can be a positive force for SBM. Large districts often benefit from centralized grant planning and appropriations. Administrators in this area acquire worthwhile resources for the schools. Nevertheless, to the advocates of on-site control, these efforts could be perceived as either a blessing or a bane. Some principals in St. Louis can, and do, solicit outside funds for their schools, but most proposals for program acquisitions must be funneled through the district's development office for approval. This is another hurdle that adds time and paperwork, but it's not insurmountable for those who know the intricacies of how to get things done within the system.

Centralization for cost efficiency is another element of school operations from which advocates of SBM cannot retreat. Large districts benefit from central-office standardization and streamlining in the areas of purchasing and warehousing, information technology, transportation, maintenance, finance, food service, security, and similar areas. Many noninstructional functions are best provided by the "downtown head shed" as it oversees districtwide services and monitors individual school budgets.

Smaller districts in many states have capitalized on centralization too, and established cooperatives to merge business functions. The cooperatives apply the economies of scale available to larger systems that would be impossible for each of the small districts to achieve if acting alone. For example, in the Dallas, TX, area, a countywide cooperative provides shared transportation, counseling services, information technology, and other supports to 15 separate school districts. Such large-scale efforts to achieve cost effectiveness at the school level require joint decision making and interdistrict collaboration.

Because effective SBM calls for joint decisions at the school, the principal must have faith in distributive leadership. Staff members, parents, and community members decide together how to advance the interests of students, which should ultimately benefit the school's academic outcomes. St. Louis's SBM facilitator noted one dimension of this philosophy that relates to, but goes beyond, fundraising issues: "SBM councils work at getting teachers to *stop* doing things that are not connected to student achievement. . . . You need to see results with children that you can validate and verify." If discretionary funds are applied haphazardly in program areas that produce no improved academic outcomes, adjustments need to be made at the school level.

In the late 1990s, for example, St. Louis identified schools that were not meeting standards on the state performance test. Special funds were allocated for teacher training and materials to implement instructional reform models. Under the SBM umbrella, each school had the opportunity to select its own model from a list that included such programs as Co-Nect, Direct Instruction, Modern Red Schoolhouse, and Success for All. After implementation of the models had begun, however, some schools found that they had to make changes because of the principal's retirement or move, staff turnover, ineffective services from model providers, or poor outcomes. In these cases, schools selected other models and redirected funds within their budgets toward other, more workable programs. If financial infusion gets no results, your SBM script needs rewriting.

For a number of St. Louis schools, community financial awareness generates support from local businesses. Sometimes a principal or an ad-hoc, on-site committee explores grant opportunities. More often in big districts, large acquisitions and long-term programs flow through the central office. Resources can take the form of computer equipment, learning materials, school uniforms, or even entire school programs.

In one case, substantial corporate and foundation funds were infused into a project at a St. Louis elementary school. SBM is a centerpiece in its design. The goal is to stabilize the neighborhood, increase community participation in the school through adult learning, meet special staffing needs, expand technology-enhanced instruction, upgrade building facilities, and improve achievement (Danforth Foundation, 2000). In the face of limited funds and heightened demands to improve academic outcomes, SBM can be the springboard for acquiring ideas and resources from corporate and foundation backers.

DO GREATER RESOURCES ENSURE IMPROVED OUTCOMES? ONE SCHOOL'S STORY

The Jefferson School project is part of a larger initiative, or compact, being implemented to improve the quality of public education for the children living in and around the Jeff-Vander-Lou neighborhoods in the city of St. Louis, MO. Jefferson School represents a set of ideas that a nationally recognized urban developer, the president of a St. Louis-based firm, believes will turn schools and communities around. The developer is known for designing innovative and affordable housing in declining and abandoned urban neighborhoods. The firm's holistic approach advocates mixed-income dwellings designed for the inner city.

These developments provide a variety of living arrangements that are architecturally interesting and contain upscale amenities.

Because uplifting the community is a critical element in the mission of the St. Louis urban development firm, it sees high-quality neighborhood schools as extremely important. The public school as a center of neighborhood activities can be crucial to stabilizing the community and joining citizen/parent involvement with business/corporate financial support.

Corporate angels for public schools are perhaps somewhat easier to locate in states like Missouri, where the state legislature has provided a Neighborhood Assistance Act that facilitates educational initiatives. Essentially, corporate donors with state income tax liabilities receive a credit, currently greater than 50%, against their tax liability when they fund projects like the Jefferson School initiative. When the federal charitable tax deduction is factored in with the state tax credit, the corporate sponsor's cost is a little less than 25 cents for every dollar given in support. This is good business for the corporate sponsors and serves to increase funds coming into the schools.

Backers of the Jefferson concept suggested that it become an example of what is needed to improve instruction and student achievement for the cluster of 10 public schools that make up the compact in St. Louis. In this case, "what is needed" comprised an infusion of more than $3 million in corporate and foundation funds into Jefferson School. It's reported that about $12 to $14 million in corporate and philanthropic resources will go into the entire neighborhood effort.

The monies for Jefferson were slated to provide a well-trained staff, the latest technologies, comfortable facilities, improved teaching, increased community and parental involvement, and expanded early childhood services. It was anticipated that these resources would result in improved levels of student achievement. Advocates of the Jefferson concept identified the following components in the program:

- A neighborhood school philosophy of active parent and citizen involvement, which includes an adult computer training center with linkages for job placement; on-site child-care and latchkey programs with links to family health-care and social services.
- A site-based management philosophy.

- A local business/corporate funding agency for infusion of developmental dollars to improve facilities, instruction, and achievement.
- A strong technology component for computer-enhanced learning with a technology support staff member on site.
- An emphasis on infusion of the creative arts to complement regular instruction.
- A school staff with commitment to deliver effective instruction, communicate with parents, and implement a program based on the Jefferson concept.
- A focus on improved student behavior and an enforced policy of no tolerance for student fighting.
- An early childhood center with a full-service preschool and on-site links to health and parenting services.

Once only a dream within a school community, corporate and foundation funds made the above resources a reality. But can corporate and foundation funds guarantee that improved academic outcomes will result?

The Jefferson project got off to a slow start in 1998–99. In the fall of 2002, the urban developer and the principal of Jefferson pointed to issues they believed had contributed to the lack of positive movement by Jefferson's students on the state performance test. Problems included a program that was not implemented until well into its second year. Then pupil/teacher ratios rose in 2001–02, reportedly increasing from 20:1 to 25:1. The staff experienced turnover, especially at the state-tested third and fourth grades. The student mobility rate, that is, students entering and leaving the school, was relatively high. The "full service" preschool was not developed to the degree that was planned. And finally, while the program did not require adoption of a specific instructional model, the reading model chosen by the principal was only halfheartedly embraced by some of the teachers.

Seven years of indicators (1995–2002), three years before the program and four after, provide a partial picture of the outcomes for Jefferson. Indicators were examined for enrollment, student attendance, the percentage of students who received free and reduced-cost lunch (SES indicator), parental participation, and student mobility. Table 4.1 shows both the three-year pre-program and four-year post-program averages for Jefferson School's selected indicators.

Table 4.1. Jefferson Elementary School Indicators during Seven School Years, without Program 1995–1998 and with Program 1998–2002 (Based on Data from St. Louis Public Schools, Annual Report to the Community, 1995 through 2002).

School year	Enrollment	% student attendance	% free & reduced lunch	% parent conference	% student mobility
1995–96	352	90.8	99.0	47.0	32.9
1996–97	340	92.1	98.8	70.0	44.7
1997–98	385	92.4	99.2	59.0	50.4
3-yr. avg.	359	91.8	99.0	58.7	42.7
1998–99	397	91.6	98.7	66.0	33.2
1999–2000	330	93.9	98.5	76.6	38.2
2000–01	343	92.0	98.0	58.0	30.1
2001–02	376	94.0	95.0	80.0	29.0
4-yr. avg.	362	92.9	97.5	68.7	32.6

In table 4.1, Jefferson School was without the corporate/foundation-funded program from 1995 through 1998 and with the program from 1998 through 2002. Student enrollments and the percentage of students in free and reduced-cost lunch remained fairly consistent during both periods. Comparing pre- and post-program averages, an overall increase in parental participation (+10.0%) and an increase in student attendance (+1.1%) occurred. A decrease in the student mobility rate (−10.1%) was also apparent. While these changes arguably are not dramatic after four years of fostering a neighborhood urban-development program, a positive trend may be emerging. Time will tell.

The most important indicator, however, is student achievement. At Jefferson, state performance test scores for the grades tested, third and fourth, from program inception in 1998–99 to 2001–02 (four years of data) showed no overall improvement until the spring of 2002. Scores remained static for the first three years of the program. In 2002, Jefferson outcomes on the high-stakes state assessment showed a 5% or greater increase into the top two levels of the test in communication arts, mathematics, and social studies and a 5% or greater decline in the bottom two levels in communication arts, science, and social studies. Even with this improvement, however, more than two-thirds of Jefferson's students continued to score in the bottom two levels on the state performance test into 2002, well below districtwide averages.

In search of positive achievement outcomes that were more representative of the program, a stable group of Jefferson children was sought. A consistent cohort of students (preschool through third grade) was identified. These were students who attended Jefferson for three years from 1998–99 to 2000–01 without leaving the program. From among a group of 343 students, just 136, or 39.7%, attended Jefferson consistently as an ongoing cohort. State test scores for 2001 in grades three and four for the above cohort, when compared to a similar group of Jefferson students who did not attend for the full three years, showed no differences in test outcomes.

Nonetheless, there is always the hope that sustained effort, correctly applied, will prove out with positive academic change. While it's too early to say for certain, improvement appears to be on the horizon for Jefferson. The school's spring 2003 state assessment scores showed dramatic improvement across all major subject areas. As indicated in table 4.2, Jefferson School scores for third graders (communication arts and science) and fourth graders (mathematics and social studies) revealed a large proportion of students who moved out of the bottom two levels of the test, step one and progressing, and into the middle level, nearing proficiency. A sizeable number of Jefferson students also entered into the top two levels of the test, proficient and advanced. This serves to reiterate that the successful application of resources and programs often takes time. Patience and the right combination of staff are essential ingredients in seeking overall school betterment.

Beyond student achievement outcomes, a tangential component in Jefferson's program is to increase the effective use of computer-assisted instruction and computer-enhanced learning. One aspect of the application of technology is the school Web site, set up at Jefferson by its computer support staff. Much helpful information for students, school staff members, and parents can be made available on classroom Web pages. But in many schools across the nation, Web-page materials are often outdated. Three years into the program, Web-page development at Jefferson didn't function at maximum utilization. Most pages remained underdeveloped and ineffective, a situation not unique to this urban school.

The principal of Jefferson noted that "some teachers lag significantly behind their colleagues" in developing abilities to use the technologies available to them. Indeed, the concept of classroom Web pages and other applications of technology appear to have been placed on the backburner in more than a few schools. Once again, this shows that ad-

Table 4.2. Jefferson Elementary School State Assessment Program Outcomes 2000–2003: Percentages of Students in Grades 3 and 4 Scoring in Test Levels (Based on Data from St. Louis Public Schools, Annual Report to the Community, 2000 through 2003).

Spring Test Results	2000	2001	2002	2003
Grade 3 Communication Arts				
% Top 2 Levels	5	2	7	9
% Mid-Level	29	26	25	46
% Bottom 2 Levels	65	73	69	45
Grade 3 Science				
% Top 2 Levels	4	2	4	33
% Mid-Level	26	24	32	39
% Bottom 2 Levels	70	74	64	18
Grade 4 Mathematics				
% Top 2 Levels	0	2	7	18
% Mid-Level	20	31	24	57
% Bottom 2 Levels	80	66	69	25
Grade 4 Social Studies				
% Top 2 Levels	2	0	5	15
% Mid-Level	3	16	14	38
% Bottom 2 Levels	96	84	80	47

equate and ongoing professional development is essential for staff buy-in and use of any educational innovation.

Perhaps the most important start-up feature of the Jefferson project is its strong effort to create close ties to the neighborhood. Significant too is the provision at the school site for lifelong learning through accessibility for citizens to adult education facilities and job placement services. In response to these measures, parent participation and student mobility rates at Jefferson could possibly be on the road to improvement. While an unacceptably large majority of Jefferson's students in 2002 were stuck in the lowest levels on the state performance test, test outcomes for 2003 began to show the fruits of the labor and the resources invested in raising levels of student achievement.

For purposes of funding educational programs, the most heartening element in the Jefferson concept appears to be the availability of outside funds to improve school facilities, instruction, and learning. As the St. Louis-based urban developer who heads up the Jefferson experiment expressed it, community donors are there to provide "what is needed and what will work."

Nonetheless, in many urban school systems today, a prime question continues to perplex educators: "What *will* work?" The school-based practices examined here may provide the foundation on which to begin to construct viable answers. The bottom line, however, is that the staff members in individual schools must be able to creatively and effectively apply these school-based strategies. Moreover, school boards, district administrators, and teachers' unions must work cooperatively with the community in order to make progress and achieve real results.

In the final analysis, the abilities and the dedication of the people controlling the school's purse strings appear to be as critical to academic success as the dollar amounts in the purse. It's not how much money you have; it's what you do with it that counts.

It's clear that the fiscal, managerial, and achievement issues that affect public education are placing greater pressures on schools and introducing more obstacles for educators to circumnavigate. To sustain worthy programs, school leaders need to continually find new sources of money as well as the expertise it takes to manage multiple fundraising endeavors. In meeting this challenge, there are many routes available for gathering resources and securing educational supports. One that continues to show promise, examined in more detail in the following chapter, is the creation of ongoing school partnerships with private corporations and especially public institutions.

THE GREAT ESCAPE

Securing funds for school programs is a lifeline to educational survival. It takes a lot of money to effectively educate today's youth and provide them with the abilities the world will demand. But can resources alone surmount the challenges that confront public education?

Consider this occurrence. A principal and a visitor are observing classroom instruction and making their rounds through an inner-city school. A discussion ensues about resources.

The 65-year-old building lacks some essentials but affords a haven from the currents that rage around it. Most students who attend the school receive a free or reduced-cost breakfast and lunch. Some arrive every morning lacking adequate sleep. Half are below grade level in reading skills, one-fourth have been diagnosed with special needs.

Tongue-in-cheek, the visitor asks, "Ever see the movie *The Great Escape*? Actor James Garner is the Scrounger. He begs, borrows, steals, and blackmails what's needed to get the job done. POWs are depending on him to break free."

"What's your point?" the principal asks.

"The kids in this building want to escape. They need the opportunities that a good education can provide. Whether they show it or not, they want to break free from their constraints. And they're depending on you for help."

"That's a far-flung analogy, even from a movie buff," the principal chuckles. "You've gone out on a . . ."

Sharp pops invade the building from the street beyond the playground. The intrusive noise, a somber recollection for some, is punctuated by a chorus of shouts and screeching tires. Attentive learners spring from school desks and blackboards to peer through barred classroom windows.

Clutching a cell phone, the principal dials 9-1-1. The school security guard who monitors the metal detectors at the entrance to the building rests a nervous hand on a holstered sidearm.

The discussion about resources is shelved. It pales in comparison to the scene outside.

ARE EDUCATION'S "INNOVATIONS" REALLY NEW?

It's hard to read a newspaper, watch television, or tune in a radio without news of America's educational plight. Ideas to make us globally competitive run the gamut from kindergarten to college. But some education innovations verge on reinventing the wheel.*

Take business partnerships with schools. It's said we must rekindle our work ethic and improve productivity. So to help kids learn about careers, a St. Louis elementary school linked up with an international corporation not long ago. Classroom teaching is combined with visits to work sites. Educators see this as a new way to stress the importance of work to schoolchildren.

---

* This section is adapted from Kedro (1992).

But what's new? Career education thrived 60 years ago. As part of their schooling, California elementary students in 1940 helped to create a model town. Businesses stocked the grade school's store and chalked it up to advertising. Children held jobs and were paid in stage money. They studied occupations from banking to street cleaning. Their principal declared, "Children should learn by experiencing something of the problems they will face when grown."

Today educators say schools must be an integral part of their communities. But 60 years ago a high school in North Carolina was already serving as a community "clearinghouse." Local residents were encouraged to bring their problems to school. Students furnished services from musical entertainment to soil analyses. The school charged no fees, and high school youth got valuable experience in solving real-world problems.

Item: youth need technical know-how to function in our 21st-century world. Yet, 60 years ago, vocational training flourished. In a midwestern high school, students in the building trades erected houses (even an addition to their school). Building one house and doing class assignments occupied the school year. Partner businesses deferred payment on land and materials until projects were sold; profits went to the school.

Today educators say schooling must be relevant to life. But during the Great Depression, junior college faculty in Columbia, MO, already had formulated useful, hands-on instruction. They also taught study skills, including how to listen and concentrate. Up-to-date audiovisuals enhanced their teaching. Traditional subjects were adjusted to the realities of students' lives. "Students learn by thinking and doing," remarked a 1939 observer, "not by listening passively with notebooks ajar."

Today teen pregnancies and aid to families with dependent children sap our economy and pose a dilemma to educators. Yet, 65 years ago a commentator warned, "More than ever, sex stimuli surround the adolescent." Nevertheless, a 1930s school committee in New York found sex instruction inappropriate. They said it awakened in kids an interest for which they weren't ready. Ironically, a home for unwed mothers was admitting two girls per month from their school. In words that might describe some contemporary school bureaucracies, a 1939 reporter found an "emotional Victorian fog" clogging our educational system. His advice: schools should teach protective sexual knowledge to develop "health and happiness for our growing generations."

Meeting the need for sexual education, another innovation that has been reinvented today, already existed in 1940. An on-site nursery in a Brooklyn high school provided 40 infants as "textbooks for the girls." In a child-care laboratory, students also learned prenatal care. "Even a career woman needs to know how to bring up children," said an onlooker.

Burdened by discipline problems, schoolteachers today are clamoring for morals education. Yet, 60 years ago, teaching values was critical. Helped by city officials, black youth in a 1930s Pittsburgh slum tackled gang problems. Youngsters elected a council and were given meeting rooms and a gym. They had their own court. With justice dished out by kids to kids, the program cut delinquency and increased self-esteem. A writer in 1940 said, "This growth in America of self-governing communities of youth is significant at a time when the responsibility of the adult citizen for the character of government is being questioned."

Recent innovations in education suggest school reform runs in cycles. We might ask: Does history repeat itself? But other issues come to mind. Over the past six decades why have educators lost sight of these "innovations"? And if some of our educational remedies are more than half a century old, can these reinventions be long-term solutions to today's problems?

CHAPTER 4 SUMMARY

To secure resources that will improve student successes, it's imperative that you understand the key financing issues that play a part in education. The SBM team should know the details of budgeting, purchasing, payroll, human resources, and fiscal reporting. The team should be aware of the costs attached to all school programs. Most importantly, the school leaders must be able to identify and go after funding sources that can provide the specific resources the school needs.

A variety of opportunities are available to acquire resources. Local money-making events can cover short-term needs. Getting long-term developmental funds or designing grant proposals for large projects are other matters. Managing sustainable funds takes a combination of strategies that attracts multiple resources. Try to garner assistance from federal, state, local, and private sources. Successful funding of school programs is best accomplished without excessive reliance on any one strategy. Don't put all your eggs into one basket.

Socioeconomic conditions in your school's community will affect the methods you'll use to raise funds at the local level. Be prudent in how often you approach parents and members of the community for financial support. Follow a fundraising plan, educate the school community about your school's need, and take steps to win community support before embarking on your fundraising mission.

A local education foundation can be of immense support to a school system in bringing in large dollar contributions. The LEF attracts a broader base of donors when it has a nonprofit 501(c)(3) tax status, because this allows contributors to use tax deductions when making grants. If your school district doesn't have a LEF, examine the possibilities of setting one up.

Grantsmanship is painstaking work. After you've determined your school's need, thoroughly research funding sources before you choose one. Write your grant proposal only after you've completed all of your homework. Prepare the proposal with readability as a guidepost. Follow instructions implicitly. Develop a strong working relationship with the granting source, and evaluate and report on your program to reassess needs and secure sustainable funding.

Finding resources will require maintaining a balance among diverse, sometimes conflicting, interests. Compromise is essential. The SBM entrepreneurial team that puts together diversified funding packages also maintains stable school programs. Exercising selectivity among program choices protects resources. Don't dilute your funds among disjointed efforts that lack systematic connection. A coherent instructional framework should be your top priority.

Sustaining multiple supports and achieving coherence requires deep collaboration on the part of the SBM team. A trusting school climate is a prerequisite to securing lasting resources for your school. But to accomplish long-term results, individual SBM teams, school boards, district administrators, and teachers' unions must work cooperatively with the community.

Ultimately, it's the people who control the school's purse strings at the school level who will be most accountable for achievement outcomes and the key to academic success. When the dust settles over school reforms, it's not how much money you've accumulated that matters; it's what you've done to reach your goals with the resources at your disposal.

CHAPTER 4 REFLECTION AND DISCUSSION

1. Describe diversified funding as it applies to a school. Why is a diversified funding portfolio crucial to maintaining and sustaining effective school programs?
2. What steps can the SBM team and school staff members take in winning community support for fundraising efforts?
3. What is a local education foundation and how can it affect the acquisition of resources for public schools?
4. What are the essential steps to take in seeking grants for your school? What should a well-thought-out grant proposal contain?
5. Why is a trusting school climate important for attracting outside funds into a school?
6. How can adequate funds improve student achievement outcomes? What is critical to the application of funds? Discuss the elements that you believe should be in place in a school to accomplish educational excellence.
7. Is there a school in your district, region, or state where corporate and foundation funds have been applied to instructional innovations? What do you know of the school's program? Prepare a case study of the school, examining its achievement outcomes in relation to the dollar amounts invested.

CHAPTER 5

Partnering for Progress

Baseball fans likely know about a pair of zany brothers, pitching partners who achieved incredible fame during the Great Depression while playing for the St. Louis Cardinals. Jerome "Dizzy" and Paul "Daffy" Dean hailed from the Ozark Mountains. The duo won national popularity as they helped the "Cards" win the 1934 World Series.

In the 1952 film *The Pride of St. Louis*, actor Dan Dailey gives a credible performance as strikeout champ Dizzy Dean, who became a play-by-play radio announcer after retiring from the mound. At one point in Dizzy's broadcasting career, St. Louis schoolteachers went after the countrified sportscaster because of his colorful mangling of the English language. Dizzy Dean's enjoyable, homespun sports talks were said to negatively affect schoolchildren. (In fifty years, how the world has changed.)

Dizzy and Daffy formed an extraordinary partnership. Finding humor in almost everything they did, they excelled in their sport and uplifted one another. As "pardners" sometimes do, they unabashedly boasted their successes. In a September 1934 double header, brother Paul pitched a no-hitter in the second game after Dizzy had hurled a shut-out in the opener. Said Diz to Daf, "Iffun yaw'd only a-told me ya wuz gonna pitch a naw-hitter, I'da pitched me one, too."

Like the Dean brothers, schools that partner with local businesses, universities, and cultural institutions should publicly celebrate their joint accomplishments. If your school is going to compete in the educational World Series, it helps to have an unswerving, positive mindset. Dizzy and Daffy believed in themselves and in each other. Your school partnerships should be premised on a plan whereby educators and community supporters "just know" they will produce a winner.

Relationships that grow out of partnerships can be as significant as your school's diverse funding portfolio in helping to sustain worthwhile school programs. A successful partnership that brings resources into your school requires collaboration and regular attention to program goals and funding allocations. Partnership strategies should remain focused and consistent, with time set aside for regular review of objectives and outcomes. Periodic discussion that centers on assessment and evaluation information will keep partnership participants aware of achievement issues that may need attention. When school conditions or circumstances in the community change, the partnership must be able to modify its support tactics to reflect new educational needs.

For a partnership to function well, the SBM leadership team, school staff members, and the representatives of the partner institution should be able to work well together. This requires individuals who understand the school community, have a broad perspective and appreciation for diverse cultural issues, and can bring a cooperative spirit and sense of humor into the relationship. Competent partnership staff are results oriented, can eliminate barriers to progress, and, perhaps most importantly, think creatively.

In some circumstances, the partnership may wish to recruit volunteers to assist with the program's delivery of services. Before volunteers work with children, be sure the participants meet basic school-system requirements that involve safety and security checks. Volunteer interns and trainees have much to contribute, but they require special attention from the school's program staff. Ongoing training of your program's volunteers is essential to impart the skills and behaviors that are critical to achieve the objectives of your school's program.

School-linked partnerships that rely on local volunteers—parents, senior citizens, high school students, businesspersons—create opportunities to expand the base of support for the school mission. But to sustain volunteer involvement in the partnership, it's important to regularly recognize and reward those who contribute their time, expertise, and concern. The SBM team can play a leading role in assisting and acknowledging volunteer partners. Use regular recognition programs and positive public relations campaigns that involve the local media.

WHY PARTNERSHIPS?

Although your school's fiscal appropriations may be more than adequate, it's still a wise decision to cultivate a variety of partnerships. However, as you gather partnership resources, linkages should be fashioned to produce a set of seamless academic strategies. Never lose sight of your school's coherent educational mission, and make certain that partnership activities are aligned with it. Carefully match resources with student needs and academic goals. When you know that the partnerships you establish will not pull your academic objectives off track, the financial, volunteer, and in-kind contributions and materials that partnerships bring to the table will serve to enhance the school mission.

By the early 1990s, more than 200,000 American businesses had set up partnerships with tens of thousands of public schools. Certainly, caution must be exercised in the creation of corporate-school partnerships. Some nonprofit watchdog groups, such as the Center for Science in the Public Interest (CSPI), have issued warnings about the infusion of corporate advertising and marketing into the schools. Nonetheless, well-structured, monitored alliances with community business interests can produce useful academic results.

Corporations can initiate career awareness partnerships or establish adopt-a-school projects. For example, numerous corporate-school linkages have functioned effectively in St. Louis's schools. Automobile manufacturers, airlines, and other business entities have developed long-standing volunteer and support relationships with individual school sites, just as they have in school districts across the nation.

Similar to corporate support from the private sector, the involvement of community institutions and faith-based organizations with public schools provides assistance to instructional staff, and it can raise the aspirations of students. Considerable research says that communities should build alliances with schools as an investment in future success. School partnerships with organizations can bolster entire school systems without burdening district or school financial obligations. Community resources can also provide programs that give wider learning experiences and positively impact student socialization.

Partnerships can be especially effective in educating disadvantaged children. In its 2001 report calling the community into action, the civic group FOCUS St. Louis reiterated a long-standing recommendation: "Develop cooperative learning partnership programs within and among school districts and universities to ensure that all students have the opportunity to learn with students of different racial and ethnic backgrounds." Earlier the Confluence St. Louis Task Force on Public Education and Economic Development noted that "higher-order skills are required for success in the workplace," and "the public-private sector must take an active and sustained role in improving education" (1989).

The Carnegie Council on Adolescent Development stressed the need for partnerships between communities and schools in *Turning Points: Preparing American Youth for the 21st Century* (1989). In *Investing in Our Children* (1985), the Committee for Economic Development advocated that schools should use partnerships to provide experiential and extracurricular learning for disadvantaged children.

School partnerships with community institutions that bring students of different races and backgrounds together in multicultural learning teams can contribute to positive relations. Research has shown that racial integration practices in education that most consistently affect attitudes are those involving students in structured interaction. Students in cooperative work groups and in one-on-one contact can have strong effects on improving racial perceptions and academic outcomes.

When community institutions take an active interest in their public schools, they provide supplemental educational materials and learning resources that enhance the quality of education. Arts, cultural, and scientific institutions can provide encounters designed to have an impact on student interest, motivation, and attitudes about school and learning. Sometimes these services are provided at no direct cost to the school system. In other cases, the partner institution's funds supplement the school system's reasonable allocations.

Along with their positive effects on student socialization, hands-on experiences outside classrooms can help pupils acquire new learning strategies. These techniques can complement the academic skills developed in school. A fuller repertoire of learning tools helps students facilitate information acquisition during their school years and into adulthood.

For example, scientists and mathematicians have long stressed that among several community institutions, science museums can collaborate with and contribute to the improvement of science and math education in public schools. Students gain motivation and understanding about applications when they see how scientific concepts are related to the work-a-day world. Teachers gain new and updated ideas and meet colleagues in science through partnerships with museums and other scientific agencies.

Partners can work jointly with teachers to formulate lessons and create materials that infuse workplace knowledge into the classroom. Students may become more motivated to learn after being involved in real-world use of their classroom knowledge. When they participate in partnership activities in nonschool settings, students can apply what they've learned. Just as importantly, they can see the relevance of their schooling while interacting with a variety of positive adult role models.

U.S. Department of Education reports have often said that programs successful in developing the talents of disadvantaged students share important features. Among the common characteristics are enrichment field trips, hands-on learning, museum visits, and projects that have application to real-life situations. Community resources can be applied to accomplish these activities and to help educate students to their fullest potential.

The challenge put forth to communities—that they support and become involved in their public schools—has been on the nation's educational agenda for decades. School leadership teams must reach out to the community to establish meaningful partnerships that benefit students as well as the partner institutions.

AFFILIATIONS WITH CIVIC, CULTURAL, AND SCIENTIFIC INSTITUTIONS

School systems and individual schools can establish highly beneficial partnerships with local museums and institutions that support cultural, artistic, and scientific educational endeavors. For example, during the 1980s and into the 1990s, a number of innovative educational supports improved racial relationships and expanded joint educational opportunities and achievement for African American and Caucasian students in the St. Louis public schools (SLPS). Multiple educational concepts were authorized under a federal court-ordered desegregation settlement agreement monitored by a court-appointed committee.

One of the most promising features of the numerous educational supports in St. Louis during those years was the SLPS Partnership Program. In large school districts it may be preferable to select and assign staff members to organize, coordinate, and monitor the resources available from multiple partnerships. The SLPS Partnership Program cultivated ties with St. Louis area businesses, universities and colleges, and local public institutions.

Among the many services coordinated by SLPS Partnership staff members were eight communitywide specialty programs, all serving the St. Louis metropolitan area. The specialty partnerships were designed, delivered, and administered by the (1) Missouri Botanical Garden; (2) Missouri Historical Society; (3) St. Louis Art Museum; (4) St. Louis Science Center and McDonnell Planetarium; (5) St. Louis Symphony Orchestra; (6) St. Louis Zoological Park; (7) United Nations Association (Greater St. Louis Chapter); and (8) Vaughn Cultural Center (Urban League of Metropolitan St. Louis).

It was my good fortune to evaluate these communitywide programs. As my collective evaluation progressed, it became apparent that the programs afforded extensive educational services that met wide-ranging objectives. Preceding the affiliation of the specialty programs with elements of the desegregation plan in the mid-1980s, each had functioned independently using private funds, but not at the same expanded levels.

Program funds were provided by the SLPS Board of Education using state monies under the desegregation settlement plan. Costs differed among programs, depending on services and activities. The district-allocated program budgets were administered by the SLPS Partnership Office. Beyond SLPS board appropriations, each institution contributed finances for staff, supplies, and student tuition. My evaluations showed program costs to be quite reasonable.

The specialty programs for St. Louis city and county schools are no longer coordinated by the SLPS Partnership Office. That office concluded operations in the late 1990s with the culmination of the desegregation plan. All partnerships eventually experience change, but the changes need not be excessively disruptive if strategies are incorporated into your plans for providing ongoing educational supports. Leadership that understands organizational history does not depend on any single entity to make a partnership work. The partnership can survive political and economic change because it orients itself to new ways of doing things and always keeps the schools and community aware of its services. For example, the above St. Louis institutions continue to provide a wide array of important educational services to St. Louis metropolitan area schools.

The main factors addressed in my evaluation of the specialty programs included purposes, levels of implementation, criteria for school/student selection and extent of participation, perceived effectiveness of racial interaction and socialization processes, and a cost analysis. Information on each program was organized around the above issues to answer the main evaluation questions: Is the program meeting the requirements of the desegregation plan? and Is the program providing useful educational services?

When the specialty programs linked with the settlement plan, their objectives began to focus on two common purposes. First, the programs fostered positive interaction between predominately black schools in the city of St. Louis and predominately white schools in St. Louis County. Black and white students worked together to accomplish learning tasks. Second, the partnerships provided enhanced, quality learning experiences to supplement regular school curricula and to align with state educational standards.

To reduce racial isolation, city and county schools that volunteered for the specialty programs contributed to integrative, growth-producing experiences for students. Nonintegrated city schools were encouraged to take part. Since integration was a sought outcome, county schools with high minority enrollments were under constraints in qualifying for desegregation funds to participate. The specialty programs contributed to a reduction in racial isolation and increased multicultural awareness.

The overviews of the St. Louis partnerships that follow are derived from my specialty program evaluations. Programs like these are worthy of replication. If your SBM team decides to create and foster links with community institutions, the information that follows may prove helpful as a how-to guide.

Within its surrounding community, every school has a local cultural, art, civic, or scientific institution that may be willing to establish a school-linked program. A local "partners for progress" initiative could benefit both your school and the institution that links with it as you work together to improve student academic outcomes and edify your community.

Missouri Botanical Garden

Ecology in Action (ECO-ACT), a Missouri Botanical Garden program, successfully imparted ecological awareness to students, promoted leadership skills in teenagers, provided useful supplements to the science curriculum, and fostered good interactions between black and white secondary and elementary school students. High school participants (Eco-Actors) studied ecology and applied their knowledge in group activities, outdoor experiences, and in teaching elementary schoolchildren what they had learned.

Program implementation was complex, consisting of multiple elements where high school students studied in groups and then paired to visit elementary schools. The tuition-free program, with its rigorous, year-long schedule for high school participants, required considerable personal commitment. Weekend high school outdoor experiences each semester included events such as caving, river canoeing, camping out, and making maple syrup at the Botanical Garden Arboretum. The six outdoor excursions (one required of a student each semester) were well-designed socialization and learning events.

Teams of St. Louis city (minority) and county high school students joined in intensive, three-week summer workshops and outdoor activities at the Botanical Garden and in the field. City and county elementary school students came together for two field trips that provided learning and personal-growth experiences.

The partnership's real-world encounters built leadership abilities in teenagers, who discussed ecology with elementary schoolchildren for about one hour per week during the regular school year. A high school student remarked, "The grade-school children like being taught by older kids, and they love the many hands-on activities the Eco-Actors bring with them." High school participants had the last period of the school day scheduled for ECO-ACT in order to plan lessons and assist in the elementary schools.

ECO-ACT was designed to meet several state core competencies in elementary-level science. Well-conceived lesson plans were provided for high school Eco-Actors and classroom teachers. Topics covered the food chain, biological communities, pollution and waste, conservation, and service projects. Sequential lessons for the elementary schools encompassed the skills of observation, classification, inference, measurement, descriptive communications, and predictive techniques applied to the environment.

During the time when I examined it, ECO-ACT served more than 550 elementary and high school students annually with desegregation funds. About one-fourth of the total funds were from Botanical Garden sources, which helped to cover fees associated with staff salaries, consulting services, student transportation, and tuition aids.

When participating teachers were surveyed, a majority of respondents praised ECO-ACT for its experiential learning and beneficial socialization activities. Among the high school student respondents, more than 80% believed that ECO-ACT developed cooperative social interaction and improved their communication skills. Moreover, the Botanical Garden program was chosen as a model in science education by the National Science Teachers Association.

Missouri Historical Society

The Missouri Historical Society is located at the History Museum in St. Louis's Forest Park. Where Rivers Meet (named for the confluence of the Missouri and Mississippi Rivers at St. Louis) was a regional history project that had functioned for eight years before it linked with the St. Louis Partnership Program in the mid-1980s.

Designed and directed by the Historical Society's education staff, Where Rivers Meet paired St. Louis city and county seventh-grade classes at the History Museum for five consecutive weekly sessions of two hours each. In all, six city school classes were joined with six county school classes during the fall semesters. All activities occurred at the History Museum and in and around Forest Park, site of the 1904 World's Fair.

Well-thought-out History Museum activities infused several state core competencies and skills in social studies and civics. Briefly, these included place geography, how people relate to surroundings, map-reading skills, knowledge of historical events, how events are perceived differently, supply-demand pricing, and ways to research topics and interpret information. The sessions also furthered educational efforts toward racial integration among St. Louis metropolitan area middle school children.

City and county teachers who participated in the program attended a one-day orientation workshop at the History Museum. The workshop took place preceding program activities to show teachers ways to prepare their students in map skills. Once involved in Where Rivers Meet, some teachers learned of and used other History Museum programs.

Each Where Rivers Meet lesson had a distinct format and objectives. To allow for student absences, sessions were delivered independently as self-contained units. Fundamental concepts, however, could scaffold on activities from previous sessions. All trips to the History Museum ended with refreshments and afforded opportunities for student sharing and interaction.

For example, among the five weekly sessions, an audiovisual presentation focused on the 1904 World's Fair, with views of fair sites in Forest Park "then and now." The presentation employed an exercise where each student identified sites on their own "then and now" map. The learning activities were followed by a bus tour of Forest Park. Students encountered firsthand the historical sites they had viewed in the slide show and located on their maps.

Most activities paired city and county students. Artifact searches sent children scampering through museum exhibits. Students compared and contrasted facsimile household items from a 1902 Sears catalog with current-day items. They read about the 1896 cyclone that swept through their city and saw photos depicting its devastation. The seventh graders learned about Scott Joplin and ragtime music, and they sang early 20th-century songs (e.g., "Meet Me in St. Louis"). Based on activities, each classroom created a historical mural that they first exhibited in their school and then shared with their partner school for display.

Students studied their own neighborhoods through observation and questioning. They began to comprehend larger historical issues using local history and learned to look for influences from the past in their immediate surroundings. An indirect benefit resulted from the program: some students approached their parents and grandparents with questions about family history generated by museum activities, contributing to heightened family discussions.

Museum sessions were well received. Comments by city and county teachers commended Historical Society staff for lesson content and quality. A SLPS teacher said, "Each session was designed with a specific goal in mind and carried out with skill . . . [and] everyone worked well together." A county teacher noted that her students anticipated museum trips with enthusiasm, and that the program provided "excellent exposure for students." Another observed, "Many of the kids were beginning to make new friends in the small groups." Paired classrooms sometimes developed continuing, long-term relationships.

When I examined the program, it was highly efficient. During a single fall semester the program served more than 300 students in roughly equal numbers from the city and the county. School funds covered transportation, materials, supplies, and refreshments. Among the Historical Society's contributions, beyond facilities and staff, were funds for the full-day teacher orientation and a 35-page souvenir booklet for the students.

St. Louis Art Museum

The St. Louis Art Museum, located in Forest Park, developed two partnership programs, each with two separate components. Visual arts seminars and visual arts studio programs were designed to tap into each student's higher-order creative abilities. Sessions provided metropolitan area high school students with opportunities for artistic interaction and socialization. Under the direction of the Art Museum's Teacher and Youth Department, programs included an art history/art careers seminar (fall semester) and a visual arts studio (spring semester).

Upon successful completion of any of the art programs, a pupil was awarded a certificate of participation and achievement, received a one-year student membership in Friends of the Museum, and became eligible to work in the Art Museum as a paid assistant through the Museum Assistants Program. Each year about 20 students who completed an art program were hired for a part-time work experience and became assistants or resource-center aides.

Art Museum programs generally attracted motivated students who displayed specific interests in art and wanted to explore their creative potential. In order to qualify, students did not need to be enrolled in an art class at their school. The art programs catered to the individual student's own aspirations and took place entirely on weekends. Students were expected to make a commitment to attend all sessions.

In the fall, the art history seminar explored selected artists and their work from a cultural-historical perspective. During six consecutive sessions of two and one-half hours each, students learned observational and critical thinking skills. The art careers seminar introduced students to careers in the visual arts. It gave participants a chance to meet and speak with professional artists at four consecutive sessions.

In the spring semester, Art Museum staff taught visual arts studios for ninth through twelfth graders. Studio 1: Portraits and People focused on historical portrayals of the human figure. Students worked in a variety of media, learned new drawing skills, and received encouragement to create portfolio-quality artwork. Studio 2: Painting focused on color and composition.

The art programs were held on either Saturday mornings or Sunday afternoons at the Art Museum. When I assessed the program, about 250 students requested to take part, but only 80 could be accepted annually. Programs, taught by Art Museum staff, paired 40 students (20 city/20 county) each fall and each spring. From among student applications and teacher recommendations, Art Museum staff selected participants who conformed to program criteria. Student attendance at weekend sessions fluctuated between 75% and 100%. Textbooks, reimbursement for transportation, and lunch or refreshments were provided to the students.

My observations of Art Museum programs found high levels of student interest and participation. Student surveys showed satisfaction with the learning experiences. For example, on a four-point scale (4 great), students who responded rated the books and handouts at 3.9, program speakers at 3.5, portfolio information at 3.6, and group discussion time at 3.3. Typical student responses about the art history seminar included "very complete studies," "wish it lasted all year," "learning and having fun at the same time," "helped us develop our own tastes and ideas," "like the method in which this class was taught," and "really felt as if the Museum cares about the young people studying here."

Art Museum programs promoted positive student interaction. Lively student socialization occurred during lessons, short breaks, and lunch.

Typical of responses, a city student wrote: "A girl from a county school taught me that you don't have to be alike to become friends. There isn't one person in this class that I didn't like." Students took the time to view each other's work, and structured activities allowed them to comment on one another's efforts.

State funds monitored by the SLPS Partnership Program covered student transportation, printing, salaries for student aides, textbooks, art supplies, and lunches/refreshments. Art Museum funds paid for some services, including a free annual membership in the Friends of the Museum, which provided access to museum activities and showings for those students who completed a program.

St. Louis Science Center and McDonnell Planetarium

The St. Louis Science Center and the McDonnell Planetarium, in close proximity to St. Louis's Forest Park, provided educational programs for city and county students. The programs supplemented the regular science curriculum with hands-on learning experiences. Separate modules were offered in planetary science and in earth science. Most activities occurred at the Science Center. A star show at the Planetarium formed one of the lessons. The SLPS Partnership Office recruited all city and county schools that took part in the popular Science Center programs, primarily on a first-come, first-served basis.

The planetary science program, Our Place in the Universe, reinforced the fifth-grade curriculum. In six consecutive weekly sessions, each two hours long, the program promoted a working understanding of concepts relevant to the earth, solar system, galaxy, and universe. In the fall semester, roughly 300 students from metro St. Louis (12 paired classes) learned the scientific method and applied it to the earth's ecology, geology, planetary motion, and its relation to the sun and other planets.

The earth science program, Investigating the Mysteries of Our Planet Earth, complemented the sixth-grade curriculum on the composition and structure of the earth. In four consecutive weekly sessions during the spring semester, about 250 students from the city and county (10 paired classes) studied the scientific method, geologic activity, rocks and minerals, and Missouri caves and fossils.

Science programs were designed to relate to state educational competencies and SLPS curriculum objectives. Briefly, planetary science encompassed galaxies, constellations, eclipses, space exploration, environmental conditions, natural forces, matter, and the conditions for life. Earth science included the classification of minerals and rocks, pollution, erosion, natural forces, fossils, earthquakes, the earth's mantle, mountains, and geologic processes.

Faculty orientation workshops at the Science Center preceded Our Place in the Universe and Investigating the Mysteries of Our Planet Earth. Instructional packets were distributed and reviewed, and the evening workshops included a light supper. Teachers from the city and county paired their classrooms, got acquainted, and learned about objectives, logistics, responsibilities, and the teaching methods used by the Science Center's staff members.

Innovative instructional methods included audiovisual presentations, cooperative learning teams, demonstrations, hands-on activities, discussions, food snacks related to class content, student journals, and classroom experiments/projects. All Science Center sessions were paired city/county meetings at Center locations.

During lessons, Science Center teachers built on previous sessions and delivered well-planned instruction with ample hands-on learning and pupil response time. Students cooperated in making observations, identifying and classifying samples, and completing journal entries. Learning and pupil interaction continued through snack time. At the close of each session, a related science activity was supplied to the classroom teacher to use as reinforcement for the learning.

On surveys, participating teachers commented that "kids enjoy science because of the activities of this program," "the best part is the hands-on experience," "good information from the instructors," and "makes science fun for the kids and easy to teach." Most teachers wrote that the program "was well set up for interaction" and that "social interaction was done well."

I observed high levels of positive pupil interaction at earth science sessions. Approximately 55 sixth graders were seated at tables and grouped into eight, pre-arranged, racially mixed teams. Teams remained the same throughout the four sessions of the program, so that students better knew one another. When I assessed the Science Center programs, they served more than 500 students annually, with roughly equal distribution among city and county schools.

Some desegregation funds were used for Science Center program supplies, refreshments, student transportation, and the salaries of part-time staff (coordinator and aides). The Science Center paid for other services, which included printed materials and staff time used in orientations, planning, assessing, and structuring program improvements.

St. Louis Symphony Orchestra

The world-renowned St. Louis Symphony Orchestra performs in Powell Symphony Hall. When I examined the program, the symphony's Educational Concerts Office oversaw its affiliation with the Partnership specialty programs, one program for elementary schools and one for high schools. Programs paired a group of selected high school orchestra students from one city and one county school and 26 elementary classrooms (13 county/13 city).

The Elementary Symphony program served more than 550 fourth- and fifth-grade pupils annually, accommodating occasional third- and sixth-grade classrooms to fill vacancies. The learning experience took place at two points in the academic year. County schools visited the city in the fall; city schools went to the county in the spring. Once each semester, partner schools attended the St. Louis Symphony's Young People's Concert Series in Powell Hall together.

The Elementary Symphony program was designed to foster music appreciation through better understanding of the historical and cultural development of music. Significantly, as with any effective partnership, symphony representatives developed specific learning objectives for all activities. The partnership anticipated that students would develop listening skills and be able to recognize melodies, chords, and recurring passages in music. Children learned about musical expressiveness, rhythm, different orchestral instruments, and composers.

The symphony's Educational Concerts Office produced an elementary school teacher's guide. The instructional packet was created to help teachers prepare their classes for symphony activities and integrate the experience into classroom instruction. Music for the Young People's Concert was selected to support the elementary level music curriculum.

Combined city/county classes were taught by symphony docents, volunteer instructors from the St. Louis Symphony Women's Association. Docents, usually two for each class, received instruction from a local university musicologist. The volunteers learned about upcoming concert music and instructional materials that could be used in the classroom. Each paired session at a school site lasted for approximately one hour and 45 minutes.

Well prepared for the musical experiences by their teachers and the symphony volunteers, students from city and county schools gathered in Powell Hall for the Young People's Concerts in the fall and the spring. For about an hour-and-a-half at each concert, youngsters were inspired, entertained, and exposed to the music they'd studied.

In terms of preparing volunteers for activities, table 5.1 compares and contrasts "how to" and "how not to" instructional techniques that might be observed during an orchestra partnership session in an elementary classroom. In the well-structured St. Louis Symphony program, strengths far outweighed any observed weaknesses.

Table 5.1.   A Hypothetical Symphony Orchestra and School Partnership: Possible Instructional Scenarios

"How To" Strengths	"How Not To" Weaknesses
Volunteer holds student interest:	Volunteer does not relate to students:
• Use of instruments and games as attention getters • Musical selections easily heard (good sound equipment) and main themes emphasized • Music tied to contemporary scene • Key words written on blackboard as they come up in lesson	• Presentation "above the heads" of elementary schoolchildren • Musical selections hard to hear (poor equipment) and too much material covered • Music not related to the present day • Too much placed on blackboard before session even begins
Advance preparation and communication between volunteer and teacher	Lack of preparation and discussion for visit between volunteer and teacher
Welcoming technique, name tags, get-acquainted introductions	No formal welcome, no get-acquainted activity
Students from paired schools teamed as partners in regular classroom	Students from paired schools seated separately in cafeteria or gymnasium
Teacher, aide, room mothers facilitate lesson and snacks	Relatively little assistance provided to partnership volunteer
Enthusiasm and high participation rate evidenced in paired classes	Low attendance, unprepared students in either host or visiting class

The High School Symphony program was an enrichment activity that enhanced students' musical talents. About 80–100 music students from high school orchestras and bands interacted within a musical context. At four separate sessions, each lasting almost three hours, student musicians came together in Powell Hall. They were exposed to two symphony rehearsals (one classical, one popular), a panel discussion by symphony musicians on musical careers followed by a luncheon, and a coaching/rehearsal session taught by symphony musicians and the conductor.

For example, at a session that I observed, a panel of symphony musicians talked about issues that included their performance in Japan, the physical rigors of playing an instrument, time spent in practice, personal motivation, discipline, planning, familial support, rehearsing, recording orchestral music, and college/university auditions and studies. The instructive session and the questions posed by students showed high levels of interest and excited anticipation on the part of students for the upcoming rehearsal with the symphony. Music teachers and students whom I interviewed praised the program.

Partnership programs should have evaluation methods built into proposals for funding and program planning. The Symphony Educational Concerts Office conducted internal evaluations of their programs. Data included a range of responses from teachers and students who attended concerts and voluntarily completed questionnaires. Survey comments by teachers generally showed high levels of satisfaction with the Young People's Concerts. On a five-point scale (5 excellent), teachers rated the Elementary Symphony program a success (4.5) and much needed (4.9). Respondents assigned a rating of 4.2 to the volunteer presenters. Overall, teachers saw benefits in student exposure to the various forms of music, instruments, and symphonic presentations. All wished to participate again.

My observations of combined elementary school sessions found high levels of student interaction. Students usually greeted their partners at the classroom door and were seated together in pairs. Get-acquainted games and lesson materials that facilitated interaction were provided by the symphony program. Elementary teachers had developed additional interaction strategies. One group of paired students conducted an ongoing association as pen pals. At another school, the host class took the visiting city children on a tour of their entire school building and playground.

Similarly, at the high school panel discussion that I observed, students were actively engaged and they thoroughly enjoyed themselves afterward during a pizza lunch in the musicians' lounge of Powell Hall. I learned that some students from city and county schools had gotten together independently to practice duets as a result of the program.

Costs of the symphony programs were comparatively low. State-appropriated funds monitored by the SLPS Partnership Office covered student transportation, symphony tickets, materials, supplies, and refreshments. The symphony provided its own resources. These included planning time, photocopies and printed materials, musician staff time in program presentations, and the voluntary instructional services of the Symphony Women's Association.

St. Louis Zoological Park

The internationally celebrated St. Louis Zoo is located in Forest Park. Partnership program activities occurred during the fall semester under the direction of the Zoo's Education Department. The zoo program, designed to promote appreciation for wildlife, encouraged sixth- and seventh-grade students from St. Louis city and county to learn in cooperative settings.

With the zoo as a "living laboratory," students were taught about the adaptation of animals to their environment and the consequences of environmental change on animal survival. Instructional materials were aligned with state core competencies and the SLPS science curriculum. Among the program's written objectives were that students would be able to work with materials not available in the school classroom and observe live animals in naturalistic settings.

Participating teachers attended an evening orientation at the zoo before the program began. The teachers received "zoobooks," posters, leaflets, and preview sheets relating to program lessons. They were encouraged to prepare their students by discussing basic concepts prior to the arrival of classes at the zoo. This contributed to improved student understanding and participation in zoo lessons and labs.

The Zoo Program consisted of four consecutive sessions, one each week. Each session ran for two hours and 15 minutes, amounting to 10 hours of instruction at the zoo for each participant. Students from four city and four county classrooms assembled at the zoo's Living World building for lessons and discussions and for field observations on zoo grounds.

The zoobooks (*Snakes*, *Birds of Prey*, *Big Cats*, and *Endangered Animals*) that students received supported each of the four session topics: Reptiles and Amphibians, Birds, Mammals, and Vanishing Wildlife. Schools were divided into two paired city/county classes. Each class attended a presentation by zoo education staff, followed by a discussion period where staff introduced live animals. Following a snack period, a team lab activity took place on zoo grounds. Inquiry-based, cooperative learning was central to the program.

Teachers were asked to assign pupils to teams of mixed academic abilities. Teams were paired city/county and were awarded prizes based on their achievement. Usually, this collaborative learning approach worked well and facilitated student interaction. To measure individual learning and assess program outcomes, zoo education staff administered quizzes to participants (10 short, multiple-choice, content questions).

Participating teachers generally believed that the program was a positive experience. Teachers responded on questionnaires that their "students' reactions to the program were excellent." Most wrote that they "liked the grouping of city and county students into teams" and praised program design that promoted "joint responsibilities" for the students.

When I assessed the zoo program, it served a maximum of 240 students per school year. That number increased in the years that followed. Beyond state appropriations, the Zoological Park contributed some resources. These included an investment in program planning, photocopies, printed materials, and staff time.

United Nations Association (Greater St. Louis Chapter)

The United Nations Association of Greater St. Louis maintains an area resource library and office that promote the worldwide mission of the UN. The partnership that I assessed, Our World and the UN, successfully achieved interaction between St. Louis area black and white students and provided useful supplements to the sixth-grade curriculum.

The program was aligned with state competencies for social studies—listening and speaking, reading and writing, and several objectives in world geography, economics, history, and government.

Sixth graders were introduced to the UN as an organization that serves many needs in an interdependent global community. The program focused on countries of the world, cultural diversity, socioeconomic differences, human problems, human rights, conflict resolution, the rights of children, and how the UN system works. Students became aware that their world is a multicultural place where problem solving is essential for living in harmony.

Participating teachers attended a one-day introductory workshop at a local college. They became familiar with program purposes and format and met UN staff and the teachers from partner schools. Classroom teachers received a program curriculum guide accompanied by activities and lessons that supported program objectives.

UN resource teachers, employed and paid by the UN Association with state funds from the desegregation plan, teamed with classroom teachers for the UN lessons. The resource teachers visited school classrooms and taught each session. Resource teachers encouraged assistance from classroom teachers and asked that they regularly use the UN materials within the social studies curriculum. Reinforcement strengthened the program and was considered essential for lasting learning to occur.

The program's eight sessions began with an opening celebration at a local university where participating schools and classrooms gathered. Each sixth-grade class selected a nation for in-depth study as they anticipated the upcoming UN learning activities.

Each UN lesson, one hour long, was designed with its own format and objectives. To conserve transportation costs, city-county paired activities were double sessions that ran for two hours. Three of the school sessions provided integrated meetings at either the host city school or the host county school. Black and white pupils were paired in classroom activities, including student presentations.

For example, the first paired classroom lesson introduced the concept of diversity. Sixth graders explored their backgrounds and began to investigate the complexities in human behavior and social interaction. Exercises involved writing about where families had come from and making a family tree. Students listed human similarities and differences, then told about circumstances that served to make life both interesting and difficult. Briefly, other lessons focused on world interdependence, global communications, and the use of knowledge and technology to improve conditions by solving problems. Classes enthusiastically planned visits to the country they had selected for study. They became acquainted with its language, customs, and foods. Some students initiated pen pal relationships with foreign counterparts.

Other sessions explored rights, needs, and responsibilities. An important activity examined feelings about conflict as well as how to deal with conflict personally, within families, in communities, and between nations. Conflict resolution included the preparation of a personal "conflict history" profile and the role playing of responses to difficult situations. This was connected to gaining an understanding of the UN and its functions. Students ranked world issues in order of their perceived importance. The program culminated on a college campus in an areawide model UN simulation. Students worked to find solutions to world problems, wrote resolutions, and role played negotiations.

When I assessed it, the UN program served about 20 classrooms or approximately 500 students annually, with equal distribution between the targeted student populations in St. Louis city and county. Levels of diverse student interaction were high and evidenced positive outcomes.

All school principals and participating teachers who responded to a survey were satisfied with UN program content, said it benefited students, and noted that they'd like to participate again. Representative of comments, a county teacher wrote that "students seem to enjoy going to another school. Similarities and differences were noted. The city students and county students worked beautifully together." Marked differences between some city and county schools and neighborhoods perhaps lent credence to the problem-solving abilities required in a pluralistic world, concepts taught in the program.

The cost of the UN program was reasonable, and the UN Association provided some resources at its own expense. These included printed materials, classroom teacher access to UN library resources at the St. Louis location, and UN staff time in program curriculum development and planning. The desegregation plan appropriated funds for transportation, some staffing needs, lesson materials, and refreshments for students.

Vaughn Cultural Center (Urban League of Metropolitan St. Louis)

The Vaughn Center, located near the campus of St. Louis University, was established in 1977 as a cultural enrichment program sponsored by the Urban League of Metropolitan St. Louis. The Vaughn Center's mission is to increase community awareness of African American history and culture. Four Vaughn programs were affiliated with the SLPS Partnership initiative. Each was available to participants as a separate educational experience.

The first program, Eyes on the Prize, used the Public Broadcasting System's *Eyes on the Prize* film series (six episodes) to enhance student awareness of the American civil rights movement. Students from city and county high schools viewed episodes in their individual classrooms. In four joint sessions they talked about emotionally charged racial issues. Participants also discussed civil rights with local St. Louisans who had been active in the movement; they visited classes to show the films.

Students in the above program could enter an essay contest. When I assessed the program, the topic was "How Did the Civil Rights Movement Make America a More Democratic Society?" Usually about 20% of the students took part in the voluntary contest. At a closing session, the young people talked about racial issues in St. Louis and heard students read their winning essays. Prizes, gift certificates donated by a local department store ($100, $75, $50, $25), were won by both city and county students.

A second program, African/Caribbean Dance, afforded sessions tailored for middle to high school grades. City and county students from the same grade level came together in school gymnasiums or multi-purpose rooms to study the history of African dance. Students learned rhythmic patterns of steps from Vaughn Center instructors and experienced live African percussion instruments. Visual and performing arts activities, which included the study and preparation of costumes, took place at four separate two-hour sessions at city and county schools. The program exposed students to an African art form and provided a chance to explore and understand dance as an element of cultural diversity.

A third Vaughn Center program, African Culture and Cuisine, was designed for middle and high school students who had access to home economics cooking facilities. The program taught students how to prepare a variety of foods from Africa, the Caribbean, South America, and the southern United States.

In three two-hour get-togethers, students from city and county locations jointly learned about the historical influences of African cooking. They participated in the preparation of foods and experienced their own "home cooked" meals at the end of each session. The cuisine program covered African peoples and food styles, the significance of food in the world, and the similarities in African, Caribbean, and African American cooking styles. Participants received menus, recipes, and cookbook references.

A fourth program, Multicultural Filmmaking, gave middle through high school students the chance to collaborate on either a photography or filmmaking project. With help from a teacher, classes produced, directed, and edited a short film (live action or animated), or they shot, developed, and assembled a photo exhibit. Students devised a script or storyboard, made props, and performed camera work.

The visual projects focused on themes that explored and portrayed diversity, and students learned about a popular art medium from a cultural and social perspective. The number of combined city-county meetings varied, depending on teacher availability and class schedules. Usually, three paired city-county and several independent sessions were needed to create the final product. Films were viewed by participants and shared with the local media (e.g., cable TV) for wider dissemination.

Generally, Vaughn programs were lauded by participants. On a five-point scale (5 excellent), teacher respondents from city and county schools gave the programs an overall rating of 4.2, and all said they would participate again. A SLPS principal commented on the dance program, stating he most liked "the involvement of black and white students. There was fun and learning taking place." A county teacher saw the cuisine program as a positive "opportunity for the city and county students to mix and get to know each other." Multicultural Filmmaking required that "black students and white students work together," remarked a county teacher. "They needed each other and the cooperative efforts paid off."

When I examined the Vaughn programs, the Center served more than 500 students annually in roughly equal numbers from the city and the county. Under the guidance of a SLPS teacher, the Multicultural Film-making program reached another 300 middle school students in the city using Vaughn Center funds.

The Vaughn Center provided some resources to schools with its own funds. Funds administered by the SLPS Partnership Office were used primarily for transportation, program staffing needs (including part-time instructors), and materials for students.

PRINCIPLES FOR PARTNERSHIPS

In 2001, the Council for Corporate and School Partnerships (CCSP) was created as a forum for the dissemination of information to help school-business partnerships better accomplish their educational goals. The CCSP conducted research and surveys and produced a set of guiding principles for business and school partnerships.

Essentially, the principles for partnerships revolve around four primary areas crucial to any type of educational program. These are (1) the development of core values to lay a foundation for the partnership; (2) giving action to your values through effective implementation; (3) sustaining the partnership over time or providing for continuity of experiences and activities; and (4) evaluating the partnership to assess its educational value to your school's mission. Within this framework of four categories, CCSP identified eight principles. A fuller discussion of the principles can be found at the CCSP Web site listed in the references to this chapter, but the basic principals and categories are as follows:

Foundation and Core Values

- Partnerships are built on shared philosophies.
- Partnerships are mutually beneficial.

Implementation and Action

- Partnership activities are infused into school and partner cultures.
- Partnerships are guided by clear management procedures.

Continuity and Coherence

- Partnerships have support at all levels in the school and partner institution.
- Partnerships have regular communications and set expectations.

Evaluation and Assessment

- Partnerships have defined goals with measures of success.
- Partnerships are evaluated to improve services and outcomes.

CHAPTER 5 SUMMARY

Partnerships constitute a valuable element in aligning resources for academic success. Business and community institutions that are actively involved with public schools afford materials and resources that enhance the quality of education. Arts, cultural, and scientific organizations especially can provide activities that improve student interest, motivation, and attitudes about learning.

Research shows that structured educational interaction promotes racial integration among students. Partnerships with community institutions can bring students of different races and backgrounds together to form multicultural learning teams. Cooperative student teams and one-on-one contact can contribute to improved racial perceptions and academic outcomes.

Beyond positive effects on student socialization, experiential learning outside the classroom provides youth with new strategies that complement the academic skills developed in school. A wider array of learning tools better facilitates information acquisition in school and throughout life.

School partnerships with community agencies function most effectively when resources are coordinated and leveraged among a variety of sources. Partnerships require effective management among school staff members, volunteers, and partnering agencies. Ongoing collaboration and program evaluation ensure efficient operation and responsiveness to students' academic needs. Partnerships should establish a learning culture that enables both parties to benefit from the association.

For example, I found that the St. Louis Partnership specialty programs provided useful services to many St. Louis metropolitan area schools. Staff members at each program implemented learning activities that supported school curricula and state educational standards. The programs conducted annual internal assessments toward self-improvement.

Throughout the nation, many public institutions in urban and rural areas are on call to assist schools. It's up to the progressive school leadership team to take the initiative and make the linkages with these organizations. As you restructure and align resources to improve academic outcomes, your SBM team can establish partnerships that will support a coherent instructional framework and enhance the learner-centered program in your school.

School alliances with cultural and scientific community institutions can help students socially and intellectually. In partnership programs that use experiential and collaborative learning, students interact to achieve common goals. When students work together, they help each other. Often they come to better understand and appreciate one another. As educational supplements, partnership programs can serve as advocates of cultural literacy, avenues for student socialization, and suppliers of extracurricular academic activities.

Some partnerships can concentrate on creative thinking and culture-rich learning. They can teach about ethnic diversity, both past and present, and enable students to gain new knowledge and a better understanding of the shared heritage and values that draw people together. Other partnerships can teach scientific inquiry, environmental awareness, and the interdependence of ecosystems. Students can complement schoolwork with broadening scientific experiences. They can develop intellectual curiosity and gain the social skills needed for team problem solving.

The partnership experiences that your students share should support the coherent instructional framework in your school. Teachers and partnership staff members must achieve consensus on the fit of the partnership to the school mission. As with any educational endeavor, procedures are necessary for the training of instructional staff and volunteers in order to effectively utilize the partnership for student learning. Appropriate professional development is critical to the full realization of any and all school-based practices that work.

CHAPTER 5 REFLECTION AND DISCUSSION

1. What are some essential ingredients required for a successful school partnership?
2. What types of resources and services can be acquired from outside the school using a partnership framework?
3. What might a school-business partnership provide to enhance student motivation and learning that could not be accomplished in the traditional school classroom?
4. What are some critical concerns affecting partnership volunteers who interact with students in your school?
5. Identify a cultural, civic, or scientific institution in your local area and contact it to determine if school-linked educational services are available. What programs are offered? Has your school established a partnership with the institution? If not, how might your school leadership team design and implement such a partnership? What are the key issues to take into account?
6. How might school partnerships contribute to communitywide multicultural understanding and promote collaborative student learning?
7. What are the "guiding principles" of a successful partnership between a school and a local business or community institution?

CHAPTER 6

Targeting Staff Development

In the film *Planes, Trains, and Automobiles* (1987), comedians Steve Martin and John Candy play businessmen trying to make their way home during the nation's busiest travel season. Rushing to Chicago to spend Thanksgiving with his family, the straightlaced character played by Martin meets the easygoing salesman portrayed by Candy. The two match wits as they confront and overcome a string of hilarious mishaps. Bad luck trails this duo as they search for all manner of transportation resources to reach their goal. Giving and receiving ideas on how to make it home (not always good ideas, mind you) constitute their attempts at problem solving.

What's this got to do with professional development, you ask? Well, watching these guys in action reinforces the notion that many of us could benefit from training in building relationships and sharing knowledge to overcome the tension involved in change. (But this movie has a positive moral message, too, and it's a great flick to watch over the Thanksgiving holidays.)

The film's eventful sojourn follows an itinerary through Lambert St. Louis International Airport, where Martin can't make plane connections. He rents a car only to find it's been appropriated by others. Unable to catch the airport shuttle at the rental parking lot, he's forced to slush his way through snow and mud back to the St. Louis terminal, where he angrily waits in line to correct the mishap. But a lost rental car receipt bodes further trouble for Martin. When he finally reaches the bubbly rental-car hostess (actress Edie McClurg), what ensues is the most emotive, tension-relieving use of the "f word" that I've ever witnessed on film.

Let's be grateful that when we find ourselves in similar predicaments (yes, even in educational circles), it's good to know that conflict resolution training and all manner of useful professional development is available, or should be, to assist staff members in the SBM environment.

Professional development conveys multiple meanings in education, especially in terms of instructional methodologies and learning strategies. The focus here is on developing an awareness of training ideas that are conducive to the implementation of successful site-based practices. As we've seen, these practices include the acquisition and placement of resources for academic improvement.

Since the mission of the school is educating all students to assume productive roles in society, instructional matters realistically can never be separated from school concerns about adequate resources. Ultimately, all professional development focuses on student achievement. And the impact of professional development on student achievement requires ongoing monitoring and evaluation.

Given the complexity of SBM budgeting and finance, it's critical that professional development be provided to principals, SBM council members, and all staff integral to the effective operations of school programs. Training should focus on fiscal control, building management, instructional leadership, understanding change, and areas of school business.

New principals entering or moving up in the system deserve a helping hand. Without effective training, it's less likely they'll engage in activities to find effective resources or become efficient in the allocation of discretionary funds when available. In this regard, progressive school systems are laying the foundation for ongoing, targeted leadership instruction. Professional development initiatives that address leadership training are wide ranging in districts that have adopted SBM.

LEADERSHIP DEVELOPMENT

School leadership requires the honing of skills to achieve convergence in essential fiscal, physical, logistical, and technological supports. Good leadership at the school site engages students. Leadership uplifts academics, improves instruction, involves parents and community, and instills a sense of common concern and ownership. The SBM leadership team must take the initiative in pulling together diverse and divergent people and programs. Training that focuses on advanced levels of problem interpretation and solution processes provides a solid foundation on which to build.

An expert problem solver anticipates emerging difficulties and solicits an array of perspectives on problems and possible solutions. The principal as problem solver selects solution processes in line with the school mission and uses a collaborative, consultative, or unilateral approach, depending on circumstances. Decision making accommodates both short- and long-term goals in finding the correct solution process (Svede, Jeudy-Hugo, & Begley, 1996). And hopefully your decision-making processes will not be straight-jacketed by bureaucratic rules and regulations.

For example, a number of education policy makers fault fiscal decision making that dictates resource allocation with no consideration for innovative school organization. Sometimes it's the new ideas and improved processes for the way students are educated that produce the most sound achievement results. A worthwhile "results-oriented system," contends Odden (1994), "would de-emphasize regulations and focus accountability on what students actually learned."

We've found that school finances should be directly linked to enhancing and improving student learning. A myopic budgetary focus on staffing, curriculum, student seat time, and similar areas may abridge interest in learning and detract from assigning sufficient attention to student outcome data. School governance bodies, says Clune (1994), should release schools from restrictions that infringe on their ability to adjust operations toward optimal performance in student learning and achievement.

With the freedom to allocate funds and adjust programs at the school level comes the realization that your educational dollars need to be invested wisely. Leadership training should include an examination of the relationship between per-pupil expenditures and student achievement outcomes. School leaders should become informed about studies that suggest the investment of additional funds has little impact on improved student outcomes. However, know that researchers are generally divided on this issue. Some say little gain in achievement levels occurs for additional dollars invested; others claim that funds applied in the correct areas are directly related to student achievement.

For example, the Committee on Economic Development (1994) concluded that money does matter, "but only if schools are organized to use it effectively to promote achievement." Sufficient funds or alternative ways of deploying resources must get to the classroom level to improve learning. As we've seen in chapter 4, to address these needs, public school systems must move to connect with alternate sources of financial support. Funding must be developed in the corporate, community, and foundation sectors. Professional development in school leadership should account for the above issues.

One fiscal trend to be aware of, especially as it affects leadership in urban school systems, is that federal funding has stabilized somewhere around 7% of the typical school system's budget. State fiscal contributions were for a time hovering in the mid-40% range, and on the whole, local funding sources continued to slide into a decline. This means that, as districts spend more on special programs and educational technology supports, a decreasing proportion of their budgets may be allocated to facility maintenance.

Urban districts, particularly many located in the central United States, have the oldest school facilities, accompanied by a higher proportion of children in poverty. The condition of the physical plant is of increasing concern to educators, because improving student academic outcomes becomes a much greater challenge in school buildings that are obsolete and in disrepair.

Attracting and retaining highly competent teachers in a deteriorating or unsafe educational environment is also tenuous. This is a critical area to address, because research shows that inputs ascribed to the quality of schooling (good teachers, lower pupil/teacher ratios) account for significantly higher standardized reading scores.

In addition to capital to upgrade facilities, rewards to superior teachers and performance incentives to schools are two variables that can produce improvements in student achievement. Local education authorities and teacher organizations need to be educated in the techniques available to accomplish these results so they can create reward and recognition systems adapted to their unique educational situations.

Leadership development in educational finance should examine how schools are spending an increasing proportion of their budgets on special education, instructional program supports, and educational technology. Wide disparities in per-pupil expenditures exist across school districts in most states. Determining the extent of these disparities proves difficult, for formulations often ignore district size, student enrollment and residential patterns, and factors such as poverty that impact student outcomes.

In school systems where large numbers of students function below grade level, those who are at risk of academic failure require interventions that generate additional spending. Cost-benefit analyses of support-program expenditures for these students show that such educational investments often yield high returns to society. Leadership training needs to incorporate these concepts within its broader context.

A critical area of leadership training should address the needs of at-risk student populations, showing how information technology can impact student achievement as well as improve data gathering and analysis at the school level. Numerous studies report the positive effects of information technology and computer-assisted instruction on general student achievement. However, practical training for school staff in technological applications must be readily available and ongoing.

As we've seen in previous chapters, especially chapter 3, the key player in the leadership framework of the school is the principal. A 2003 report by the Center on Reinventing Public Education (CRPE) examines the school principalship and finds that different schools require different leadership styles. Not surprisingly, the CRPE study, commissioned by the Wallace Foundation, argues that effective leadership styles are not interchangeable among schools.

Principals should be placed in schools where their strongest skills will accomplish the most good. Moreover, professional development for principals should focus on those skills that particular individuals must develop in order to improve their school. Training should never follow a prepackaged, "one-size-fits-all" format. Each school has a unique set of features. The principal needs to know how to diagnose problems and create solutions specific to his or her school. Professional development should take into account that there is no single path that will develop effective leaders.

The CRPE report itemized the needs of school leaders under seven categories. These areas may be worth considering as you design targeted training programs for your school leadership team. While school leadership needs vary, the CRPE study identified the following as major factors to consider: instruction (curriculum and professional development); culture (school tone and climate); management (operating procedures and facilities); human resources (hiring and performance evaluation); strategic planning (vision, mission, and goals); external development (fundraising and partnerships); and "micropolitical" (facilitating successful interaction among the preceding six factors).

Training to Solve Tough Problems

Professional development should include opportunities to learn how to tackle complex issues that appear insolvable. Like Martin and Candy in *Planes, Trains, and Automobiles*, when we're heading for home, we may run into problems that have no apparent solutions. Sometimes getting to our destination requires changing course, taking unusual action, or using collective efforts never before envisioned. Referring to Heifetz's *Leadership without Easy Answers* (1994), Michael Fullan notes that "leadership is what you need to solve problems for which there are not easy answers" (Fullan, 2002).

In *Leading in a Culture of Change* (2001), Fullan uses theory and case studies to elaborate on the dynamics of leadership in our fast-paced world. He constructs a framework assembled from mindsets ("actionsets") composed of five interconnected fundamentals that make up effective leadership. Fullan's essential elements of leadership for sustainable change include moral purpose to make a positive difference, the capacity to understand change, relationship building among diversity, knowledge creation and sharing, and coherence making that achieves focus amidst multiple issues. These fundamentals should be covered within the context of your school's leadership training program.

Moral purpose in the above framework involves satisfaction in your accomplishments coupled with making contributions that genuinely affect others. Understanding change is the ability to develop good ideas and put them to use by interacting with and convincing people to adopt improved ways of doing things.

An insightful observation by Fullan about building relationships is that reform strategies that work improve relationships; poor strategies leave relationships static or worsen them. Good relationships contribute to creating knowledge in a school setting when information is socially processed by teachers working together to make things better (e.g., professional learning communities). And just as teachers can learn from one another within the school, knowledge can be shared across schools. Finally, creating coherence in your school does not mean taking on all ideas and problems and making sense of them in one fell swoop. Coherence is determining what's most important to focus on and being able to keep your ideas afloat on a stormy sea of complexities.

When discussing leadership styles, Fullan introduces concepts advanced by Goleman (2000) and others. Leadership styles identified by Goleman include coercive (do what I tell you); authoritative (come with me); affiliative (people come first); democratic (what do you think?); pacesetting (do as I do); and coaching (try this). Four of the leadership styles appear to be most successful in accomplishing positive movement in change and culture. These styles are authoritative, affiliative, democratic, and coaching. As we learned in chapter 3, effective leaders use each of these styles to varying degrees at different times and in different circumstances. Professional development in leadership skills should instill in the school's SBM team an understanding of these styles and other effective problem-solving techniques.

Recent work on leadership by the above authors and others in the field has extensive application to professional development for school leaders. Many studies, including Fullan's slim volume on leadership, provide important reading for any training activity that focuses on change processes.

PROFESSIONAL DEVELOPMENT AND STUDENT ACHIEVEMENT

Effective school leaders promote leadership skills at all levels of the school organization. Thus, future leaders on the SBM team are always in the process of being developed. All school leaders should keep their eyes on the ultimate reason behind professional development: improved teaching, learning, and student achievement.

In one area of school leadership, educators advocate the need for ongoing professional development in instructional innovations to accomplish the implementation of proven teaching methods and learning strategies. A variety of analyses reveal teaching practices, standards-based policies, and key professional development areas likely to result in achievement gains as students advance through the grades. Quality professional development should support instructional reform efforts, district curriculum, and state standards. It should reflect the school's change practices. Moreover, training activities should bolster teacher confidence in using the new instructional approaches.

Among the essentials for teacher preparation is training in how to provide effective instruction in small-group learning configurations. On-site workshops and in-service training develop teachers who account for each student's existing skill level when planning instruction. With consistent support, these effective teachers integrate reading instruction into mathematics, science, and other content areas (literacy-based learning), use a variety of classroom assessments, and are capable of teaching heterogeneous ability groups.

The well-prepared teacher also benefits from staff development in exploratory instructional techniques. The use of handheld technology and manipulatives to demonstrate concepts in mathematics is one example of such training. Teachers should show their students that there are multiple ways to solve problems. Teacher preparation at the school site should afford opportunities and practice in instructional strategies, including conventional presentation activities, group discussions, board demonstrations, classroom assessments, oral responses, and individualized student work.

For example, considerable research on literacy practices that produce results in middle and high schools has been synthesized by Langer (1999). In urban schools with large proportions of disadvantaged or minority students, certain characteristics are requisite for success in literacy attainment and positive movement in student achievement. Among "best practices" are several characteristics with ties to professional development. These include teacher participation in professional communities, structured teacher improvement activities, and respect for lifelong learning.

In short, professional development helps teachers keep up with current ideas and innovations in their fields. Quality teachers participate in a number of learning communities such as cross-disciplinary instructional teams. These teachers shape their work by shared decision making, team cooperation, and action research. They think of themselves as leaders, sincerely care about students and colleagues, and are committed to learning the best techniques available for educating their students. Effective teachers use staff development to introduce new concepts into their classrooms. Finally, they become computer literate to assist with ongoing, self-directed educational improvement.

A major variable affecting student outcomes is the teacher's understanding of and ability to use the available technology in the instructional process. A big investment in computer technology without appropriate staff development and service support systems is largely meaningless in terms of improving student achievement. A data-driven management system coupled with targeted staff training would identify and allow for correction of such weaknesses.

Many studies make a strong case for training that has practical application, especially for instructional staff involved in reform for academic improvement (North Central Regional Educational Laboratory, 1996). Useful staff development combines numerous goals that are essential for either incremental or systemic change. Among primary objectives, certain concepts reemerge as critical: professional development is an essential link to higher student achievement; professional development is as vital as classroom instruction; professional development is job embedded and inquiry based; professional development is clearly related to reform. (See figure 6.1.)

Nonetheless, with all of the above information at our disposal, a U.S. Department of Education nationwide survey of teachers found just 45%

Figure 6.1.   Focus Training on Achievement

able to respond that they felt well prepared to implement new teaching methods or their state and district's curriculum (Parsad et al., 2001).

Thoughts on Teacher Development

Students benefit academically when their teachers are well-versed in the subject matter they are teaching and are knowledgeable in effective instructional methods and learning strategies. Not surprisingly, teachers generally welcome professional suggestions about improving their instruction. It's imperative, however, that those who deliver staff development programs for teachers establish a logical connection between the content of the learning and the anticipated student outcomes.

Student achievement also benefits from school staff collegiality. When teachers share ideas, cooperate in activities, and help each other with intellectual growth, the school's learning climate is uplifted. Professional learning communities are established where teachers interact around student results and introduce techniques to engage students and improve academic outcomes.

In schools where teachers participate in meaningful in-service training activities and collaborate in developing useful instructional strategies, student learning improves. Conversely, lack of teacher contact during the school day and noninvolvement in development activities contribute to teacher isolation, which may thwart instruction.

Teachers should begin to learn together and assume joint responsibility for their classrooms. It's critical that school staff members discover and acquire knowledge as a team rather than separately. The organizational implication of this concept is that schools become places for teachers to learn as well as to teach.

Restructured conceptions of staff development are strongly advocated by many educators. Reform-minded practitioners say in-service activities should be changed from a deficit-based to a competency-based approach, shifting from teacher reliance on external supports to self-reliance in instructional decision making.

The administration of the school district needs to shift from a centralized to a decentralized approach for providing staff development. This involves a tilt in school culture away from staff development directed entirely by the central office toward the facilitation of in-service activities identified by teachers and implemented on site. Teachers should know what is most needed in their school to improve student achievement. If not, they must be guided into learning situations that will show them how to do this.

Progressive professional development requires not only formal training, but the adequate opportunity for teachers to learn in their day-to-day work. A teacher's instructional role can be expanded using programs that capitalize on experienced classroom teachers as educators for on-site workshops and training sessions. Adjustments in scheduling need to be provided so that teachers can use school time for reflection to develop knowledge and skills related directly to their classrooms (e.g., action research).

Professional development delivered through partnership affiliations with local universities and educational organizations is available and easily accessible to most school districts. Learning partnerships such as the programs discussed in the previous chapter should be created. Mentoring programs should link novice teachers with experienced teachers at each school site. Staff development utilizing mentoring as one component directs the professional growth of new teachers by advocating reflection, teacher collaboration, and inquiry (Smylie & Conyers, 1991; Zimpher & Ashburn, 1992; Feiman-Nemser & Parker, 1992; Darling-Hammond, 1994).

Improvements to teacher education and staff development emerged as national education goals in the mid-1990s. They remain primary issues in comprehensive school reform. There's no getting around the fact that practicing teachers are the key to the transformation of schools. Teachers should be encouraged to take the lead in school-based reform efforts; to do so, they need enriched professional development experiences.

Little (1993) identifies five factors that exert some impact on enhanced professional development: (1) teachers have time to expand in-depth knowledge in subjects taught and to acquire certification in needed fields; (2) teacher ability is developed to meet the multidimensional needs of heterogeneous classrooms to provide fairness to differing student populations; (3) the extent and use of assessments is adjusted so that a reasonable amount of formal testing is balanced with teacher evaluations of student capabilities; (4) the school social organization allows leaders to foster subject-area and grade-level team collaboration; and (5) the "professionalization" of teaching is encouraged. The last item brings to mind accomplished teaching as evidenced in certification requirements such as those advanced by the National Board for Professional Teacher Standards. Studies indicate that nationally certified teachers can raise the level of instruction throughout the schools in which they teach.

Teachers actively engaged in the above processes must necessarily rely on data that are accurate, reliable, and timely. In this regard, McLean (1995) contends that the "implementation of a complete program of data collection and use can lead to the improvement of education as has no other educational innovation of the last century." Individual student and schoolwide data ably gathered and analyzed should reveal better ways to serve students. This includes assessment of school-site culture and leadership, classroom management skills, student learning styles, and similar factors that affect student achievement. Staff development must also instruct teachers on how to analyze and use school data effectively to improve classroom outcomes.

Important Assumptions about Adult Learning

Malcolm S. Knowles, a frequently cited theorist-practitioner in adult education, is sometimes referred to as the "father of adult learning." Knowles popularized the term "andragogy," defining it in *The Modern Practice of Adult Education* (1970) as a new system, process, or emerging technology applied to adult learning. Andragogy represents an alternative to pedagogy and in some respects is a learner-focused approach that can be applied to all ages (e.g., self-directed learning versus teacher-directed learning).

Knowles recognized that adults possess an inherent need throughout life to remain useful contributors to society. We achieve our identities in part by reaching our fullest potential and applying our skills in meaningful endeavors. In all facets of life, today's accelerated pace of change mandates that adults learn and relearn; learning is a lifelong endeavor. Information and ideas acquired in one's early years quickly become inadequate. Over time, we all come to the realization that some of the skills we learned in school and college have become outmoded by newer, more efficient practices and innovative technologies.

Knowles, who first learned of andragogy in discussions with European colleagues, developed a set of assumptions that educators should remember when they create and participate in staff development programs. One of these concepts—and this should be obvious within the framework of effective school-based practices—is that teachers are adult learners who are capable of participating in the diagnosis, design, execution, and evaluation of their staff development activities. Indeed, this is one of the premises underlying teacher-led action research projects at the school level.

Andragogical assumptions about learning are built on a set of important drivers. These include self-concept, self-direction, and motivation to learn; use of prior experience and knowledge; readiness to learn when faced with new tasks; and an orientation to apply new learning to solve immediate problems. Consequently, Knowles recommended that educators who teach adults, including those who deliver professional development and in-service programs, construct a learning climate on the foundation of cooperation.

The identification of staff development needs should consider the mutual concerns of those who are to receive the training. The recipients of the training can even participate in the makeup of the activities that will be used to accomplish their learning objectives. And the learners must evaluate the quality of the learning process to determine their particular requirements for further professional development.

EVALUATING PROFESSIONAL DEVELOPMENT: A CASE STUDY

Measuring the extent of professional development in a school system, especially a large one, is complex. It's a challenge to gauge training and its effects when schools choose from among many instructional reform models in an effort to meet state standards. The task becomes more formidable when models are selected at different times and some are changed along the path toward academic improvement.

As an example, I'll discuss a practical evaluation project in which I participated as a primary investigator (Kedro & Short, in press). It may serve as a how-to guide, adaptable to your school or district, when your

SBM leadership team assesses the level of instructional training and its impact on student achievement in your school.

During 1999 and 2000, the St. Louis public schools identified sites that didn't do well on the state's high-stakes performance test. Forty schools were eventually chosen to receive extra funds for instructional innovations associated with comprehensive school reform. Specifically budgeted appropriations were provided for teacher training and instructional materials to implement the "research-based" innovations. The schools were identified as Schools of Opportunity (SOPs). The goal: to achieve state standards and earn full accreditation. A dozen different instructional models were off and running.

With such diversity in programs, how can you evaluate implementation and assess desired results? One big concern begs an answer: what did the teachers know, and when did they know it? There are other important questions as well. Was professional development adequate? Did training in the models make its way into classrooms? Were the instructional innovations of benefit, that is, did they lead to improved student achievement?

Get a Grip—Do Some Research

Before you decide on how to approach getting answers to the questions posed above about evaluating professional development, review relevant research. In this case, it reminds us that quality staff development is needed for all teachers involved in educational reform (Sparks, 2000). Staff development is an essential link to higher student achievement.

A U.S. Department of Education report on longitudinal change and performance in Title 1 schools (2001) found that teachers who gave a high rating to their professional development in reading and/or mathematics had students who realized greater achievement gains than the students of teachers who gave their professional development a low rating. A factor that affected gains was training that supported school reform and bolstered teacher confidence in using new approaches.

As discussed in chapter 3, the Council of the Great City Schools compared four urban school districts that realized academic achievement gains with districts that didn't see similar improvement. CGCS findings determined that, among a number of important factors that contribute to school performance, extensive professional development positively affects student achievement.

A review of nationwide research shows that the successful implementation of instructional models in some cases results in improved student achievement. In order to succeed, however, model strategies must be widely infused into school instruction and aligned with district curriculum and state standards. Even when effective staff development and model implementation occur, positive movement on student achievement may take three or more years.

Starting in a new direction doesn't necessarily mean quick successes will be realized. There can be potholes and detours along the road. It's imperative, then, to know if teachers have been adequately trained, and if, indeed, they are appropriately infusing the model strategies into classroom instruction.

Design a Study

To assess professional development in your instructional model, determine the questions that you need answered. Decide what will be investigated, by whom, and how.

Major questions asked in the investigation discussed here included: (1) How many teachers at elementary, middle, and high schools believed they were adequately trained in the instructional models? (2) How does the length of time with a model affect perceived training and use of the model? (3) What is the level of acceptance by teachers of the appropriateness of the models for their students? (4) Does length of time with the model, training, and perceived use and acceptance relate to cumulative outcomes on the state's performance test?

Survey—Look for Changes over Time

To gather the required data for your study, use standardized surveys that meet your needs, or design, test, and use your own instruments, or both.

For three consecutive years (2000–2002), the SLPS Research Division disseminated surveys to all instructional staff members in the schools that had implemented reform models. In the first year, a standardized, validated instrument, the Concerns Based Adoption Model Questionnaire (CBAM), was administered. The CBAM measures respondent concerns about issues that reflect stages of program acceptance (Hall & George, 1979; Hall et al., 1973). The CBAM was repeated in years two and three. At that time, however, it was accompanied by a SLPS research program-specific questionnaire developed as a check on the CBAM.

Items on the SLPS survey pertained specifically to training in the instructional models. The in-house survey categorized perceived levels of model use into five levels: nonuser, novice, intermediate, old hand, and past user.

Studies based on staff perceptions alone lack the reliability of multiple-data analyses. Nevertheless, a high percentage of respondents and consistency among responses can afford valuable information about professional development. Remember, however, that low staff response rates for individual schools or models may not provide suitable data for those particular sites or models.

Twenty-five schools (62.5%) completed and returned the surveys in 2002, whereas 36 schools (90%) had done so in 2001. Sending out surveys near the end of the school year in 2002, rather than in February, as in 2001, lessened the response rate. Timing is important.

Data from the locally developed survey were longitudinally compared for teacher responses to items concerning the instructional models. When returns were examined districtwide for each level of schools (elementary, middle, and secondary) the number of respondents (N=552 in 2002; N=715 in 2001) and their representativeness provided useful data. Analyses of the data for SOPs with three consecutive years in a model determined the extent of professional development and the degree to which the models were accepted (see table 6.1).

The spring 2002 SLPS survey indicated that 80% of the respondents districtwide believed they had received adequate training in their school's model, a substantial increase from 2001. However, the

Table 6.1. Teacher Responses in Percentages to Model Questions, Spring 2002 and 2001, by School Level, Adequate Training, Level of Use, Time Teacher in Model, and Using Alternative Model

School Level	N	Received Adequate Training (%)	Level of Use (Knowledge)			Teacher in Model		Using Alternative Model (%)
			Nonuser (%)	Novice (%)	Intermediate or Old Hand (%)	0–1 Year (%)	≥2 Years (%)	
Spring 2002								
Elementary	273	82	11	31	58	34	66	35
Middle	218	78	15	23	62	34	66	38
High	61	74	14	35	51	44	56	27
Total (weighted)	552	80	13	28	59	35	65	35
Spring 2001								
Elementary	334	56	12	52	36	77	23	21
Middle	262	72	8	35	57	34	66	22
High	119	31	25	35	40	54	46	25
Total (weighted)	715	58	13	43	44	57	43	22

use of alternative teaching strategies to the models also rose from about one-fifth of respondents in 2001 to about one-third in 2002. And while arguable, two-thirds of these teachers said their alternative strategy did not interfere with their model.

According to categories reported by the CBAM, in 2002 only a few schools appeared to be moving toward model acceptance. A longitudinal examination of the CBAM showed that most schools made no movement at all toward more complete staff buy-in. High levels of staff turnover in some schools resulted in the lack of adequate first-year training for many teachers unfamiliar with the models. This likely showed up as little or no change on the CBAM survey.

On the 2002 SLPS in-house survey, among teachers with training, 24% still reported as novice or nonuser. This, too, perhaps revealed inadequate training in some cases and resistance to the model innovations in others. Among the responding schools, just eight (32%) indicated that 70% or more of their teachers (generally an effective level of staff buy-in) saw their model as appropriate for their students. Responses to the 2002 in-house survey showed that, districtwide, 60% of respondents believed their model was appropriate for their students; 40% believed it was not.

On the other hand, in spring 2002, the SLPS survey found that the increased length of time the models were in the schools contributed to an increase in the percentage of teachers, overall, who reported adequate training. In elementary schools in 2001, 56% of responding teachers reported adequate training; by 2002, this increased to 82%. Middle and high school responses also showed increases.

In 2002, more teachers at all levels saw themselves as intermediate and old-hand users of models than had in 2001. Teacher respondents who had two or more years with a model and who said their training was adequate were more advanced in their use of the model. Length of time with the model affected increased experience.

Visit, Interview, Observe, Examine

Attempt to corroborate your survey results with visits to schools, staff interviews, classroom observations, and examination of relevant supporting documents.

In spring 2002, SOP principals and reform model facilitators participated in focus-group interviews with Research Division staff members. Principals agreed to continue with their models through the next school year. Most concurred that school staffs were supportive, although staff turnover severely hampered implementation in some schools. More time was needed with the models, said principals and facilitators, in order to gain a fair assessment of their impact on instruction and achievement.

The SLPS Division of Research developed and tested a package of observation instruments designed to rate instruction and learning in the SOP classrooms. Areas of concern focused on high-order learning, inquiry-based instruction, critical thinking skills, and performance-oriented tasks aligned with the state standards. District evaluators visited, observed, and rated the SOPs. Visits showed that the implementation of models occurred at widely varying levels across the district. Generally, schools with high ratings for implementation of their model also received high ratings for classroom instruction.

Examination of school improvement plans, prepared for the 2001–02 and 2002–03 school years by the SOPs, showed strengths at a majority of the schools. Overall, the instructional plans improved from previous years. However, a few remained too general. Some didn't link identified academic needs with data-driven instructional strategies supported by well-delineated professional development activities.

Track Longitudinal Student Achievement

Establish baseline achievement data for the program that you're studying in an effort to measure program effects. But remember that multiple factors impact achievement. Attributing change to one intervention among many may not be possible.

Outcomes on the state performance test from 1999, the baseline, through 2003 were examined for the SOPs. Longitudinal changes were calculated based on the percentage of all students who moved out of the bottom two levels of the state test and into the top two levels. This was done in the four subject areas tested: communication arts, mathematics, science, and social studies. Outcomes were determined for each of the 40 SOPs and for each instructional model. Analyses attempted to find alignments between changes in test outcomes and the reported levels of model acceptance and implementation.

The elementary schools showed the strongest overall improvement. SOPs at the middle and high school levels generally remained static on test outcomes, and no model appeared to substantially affect improvement at those levels (see table 6.2).

Among the elementary SOPs, the model that achieved the largest positive movement on the state assessment for all schools using that model was Success for All. It's significant to note that Success for All also had the highest reported level of adequate training (86%), the most respondents who reported as intermediate/old hand (73%), and the fewest who used an alternative model (20%), an indicator of staff commitment. Other elementary school models showed results, too, but none as dramatically as Success for All.

The above outcomes were obtained for a particular study in a single urban school system. The findings in your school district would be subject to the variety of models adopted and the levels of professional development and implementation for those models.

Table 6.2.   State Test Score Changes from Spring 1999 to Spring 2003 for Schools of Opportunity in the St. Louis Public Schools

School Level & Subject	% Change Out of Step 1 & Progressing	% Change Into Proficient & Advanced
Elementary (23 schools):		
Communication Arts	−15.0	+11.0
Mathematics	−11.0	+6.0
Science	−25.0	+27.0
Social Studies	−19.0	+17.0
Middle (14 schools):		
Communication Arts	−2.0	+2.0
Mathematics	−12.0	+4.0
Science	−3.0	0.0
Social Studies	−12.0	+8.0
High (3 schools):		
Communication Arts	+7.0	−5.0
Mathematics	−4.0	0.0
Science	−11.0	0.0
Social Studies	−4.0	−2.0

Make Useful Recommendations

Based on your study's findings, if recommendations are required, they should be easily understood and practical. For example, the following are two of several recommendations that emanated from this study of professional development for teachers and student achievement outcomes:

- Staff at each SOP should jointly reexamine the alignment of their instructional model with state standards across grade levels and subject areas. Staff should identify, incorporate into their school improvement plan, and implement specific steps to achieve instructional coherence.
- Adequate training for teachers new to an instructional model is essential and provision for that training requires greater attention from school site administrators, district professional development staff, and model facilitators in the schools.

The degree of professional development in an instructional model can be determined through internal self-evaluations using surveys, interviews, and observations. Improvement in student achievement should be detectable for schools with adequate staff training in a selected instructional model and effective implementation of that model. The right model practiced by a large proportion of a school's instructional staff may contribute to positive change on a state high-stakes performance assessment.

Self-assessment at the school level is essential in order to determine that your professional development is accomplishing what it is intended to do. At its highest levels, practical professional development can uncover unrealized potential, capitalize on individual strengths, and instill cohesiveness in the school workforce.

CHAPTER 6 SUMMARY

Targeted professional development should be provided to principals, SBM leaders, and all staff members critical to the school's instructional program. Fiscal control, building management, instructional leadership, change processes, and tested innovations in teaching and learning are a few of the areas worth exploring in staff development sessions. Absent such training, it's less likely that school leaders will uncover worthwhile resources or allocate discretionary monies where they'll do the most good for students.

The qualities of efficient school leadership go beyond simply controlling the purse strings. Expert leaders engage students, improve teaching and learning, and raise academic outcomes. School leaders involve parents and community in academic issues and build a sense of common purpose among stakeholders. Leadership training should encompass a detailed examination of these skills through role playing, case studies, and other experiential activities prescribed for the diagnosed needs of the school.

The key to a cohesive leadership structure in the school is the principal. But different schools require different brands of leadership, and effective leadership styles are not necessarily interchangeable among schools. Therefore, the training of school leaders should not assume that a standardized program will fulfill all requirements. Professional development must be designed to meet the unique needs of each school. There is no universal, catch-all system of training that guarantees effective school leaders.

An important aspect to any training program is that it shows school leaders how to surmount complex issues. Such a program might present studies of leadership that include Fullan's five essentials for sustainable improvement: moral purpose; understanding change; relationship building; knowledge sharing; and coherence making. And remember Fullan's observation: reform strategies that work improve relationships; poor strategies leave relationships static or worsen them.

Useful professional development that is put to work in the school and classroom contributes to higher student achievement. Successful school leaders acknowledge that staff members trained in recognized practices and provided with ongoing support improve classroom instruction. Practical professional development is best if tied to the school's instructional program, linked directly to the job, and inquiry based in nature. Training should also present a sound connection between what is being learned and the expected outcomes for students.

Targeted professional development bolsters student achievement. Students reap rewards when teachers demonstrate collegiality, are knowledgeable in their subjects, and use innovative methods that motivate learners. Teachers who share useful ideas and cooperate in professional learning communities uplift the culture of the entire school. When teachers collaborate in professional development and are active in worthwhile in-service training, student learning improves.

Several factors come together to enhance professional development. First, teachers are provided with opportunities to expand their subject-area knowledge and to earn certification in needed fields. Instructional staff members receive training to meet the needs of heterogeneous classrooms. The amount of formal testing that occurs in the school is reasonable and balanced with teacher evaluations of student abilities. Finally, the organizational structure of the school accommodates team collaboration and promotes the professional status of the faculty.

When the principal and the SBM team identify staff development needs in the school, they should consult with and consider the concerns of those who are to receive the training. Teachers pursuing new concepts through professional development can be called upon to devise the format of the training that will be employed to reach their learning goals. Teacher-learners, as well as administrator-learners, should have the chance to assess their learning in order to decide what may be required in the way of additional training to accomplish their objectives.

The degree to which professional development has affected your school can be determined in internal evaluations. Use multiple data sources, such as surveys, interviews, and observations, to determine the extent and the quality of staff training. Improvement in student achievement should be detectable over time if adequate training and effective implementation of the selected intervention has occurred.

Training in the right methods put into practice by a large proportion of a school's teacher corps can bring about positive change on high-stakes, student performance assessments. However, self-evaluation at the school level is imperative in order to know that your professional development is accomplishing what it is intended to do.

CHAPTER 6 REFLECTION AND DISCUSSION

1. Identify and define three important aspects that you believe are critical to leadership training in your school.
2. How should training programs for principals address the fact that school leadership styles vary from one school to the next? Can you provide an example from an experience in your school system?
3. What are some of the major issues affecting a school that require strong problem-solving capabilities? What is involved in finding workable solutions to these problems?
4. What are the five critical elements identified by Michael Fullan to accomplish sustainable positive change? How do these five essentials relate to school-based management and effective school practices? How would you incorporate them into a school leadership training session?
5. What professional development conditions should be in place for teacher training to positively affect student achievement?
6. Identify and describe areas of professional development that you believe would benefit your school. Is there a leadership team in your school that could assess and/or implement your recommendations for training?
7. Describe how you would go about assessing the extent, impact, and effectiveness of a particular professional development training program in your school?

CHAPTER 7

Overcoming Resistance and Unlocking Potential

Stop singing the blues and get on with becoming a success. That's one message that emerges in the movie *St. Louis Blues* (1958). The film depicts the life of songwriter W. C. Handy, and the velvet-voiced crooner Nat King Cole stars in the leading role. Some say the script of this less-than-accurate biography leaves much to be desired. But weak scriptwriting takes a backseat to the collective musical talents of a stellar cast. Legendary blues artists Pearl Bailey, Cab Calloway, Ella Fitzgerald, Mahalia Jackson, Eartha Kitt, and others perform a dozen Handy songs, including a terrific rendition of the title sung by Cole.

The movie opens with Handy's minister-father admonishing his young son for an attraction to the blues, "the devil's music." As the story unfolds, we see Handy making it on his own terms. The self-reliant songwriter overcomes a string of obstacles, including a bout with blindness brought on by stress. Ultimately, Handy discovers and nurtures his talent, conquers resistance, wins fame and fortune for his music, and even earns the respect of his father. Indeed, "St. Louis Blues," a song that Handy initially had a rough time promoting, went on to become one of the most recorded American tunes of the 20th century.

The accolades that have been bestowed upon W. C. Handy and Nat King Cole will surely surpass any kudos that might make their way into the school for the principal and the SBM leadership team. Nonetheless, school staff members can't spend valuable time singing the blues. They too must exercise high levels of self-reliance, creativity, and focus, always capitalizing on their strengths.

In an academically proficient school, the leadership team accepts complete responsibility for the school and the performance of its students. This could be tough if the school is mired in an equilibrium that discourages change. It's fairly common for school staff members to be wary of transformation. Therefore, the SBM team must develop the untapped potential of each person in the school.

The principal and faculty must come to see themselves as the drivers behind school successes. All are aware of change processes in the school and confront problems together. When setbacks occur, they look to themselves as one of the possible reasons for their students' achievement difficulties.

The directors of change in the school need to be supportive and approachable throughout the change process. School leaders must know when to stand back and take stock and when to intervene with advice, coaching, or direction. The SBM team, especially, needs to bring out the best in all colleagues, establishing the rapport and confidence that will instill a collective, problem-solving mindset in the school.

Having new ideas take hold is as much about people and school culture as it is about the innovations and methodologies that are selected to improve outcomes. Regardless of the launching point—the principal acting alone, the SBM team, or a grassroots movement of innovative teachers—success in efforts to restructure and align resources requires the pursuit of a phased-in process of implementation. Full-scale change and adoption of reforms can only come to fruition when accepted and orchestrated by the principal and the leadership team. Once the plan for change is off the ground, the entire school and its support system can begin to anticipate a positive future. And the best way to predict the future is to create it.

SLICING THROUGH BARRICADES

Effecting meaningful change that overcomes academic setbacks often runs head on into resistance. You may be attempting to succeed in a school that functions in a climate of inertia. It takes a considerable amount of training, coaching, and prodding to attack collective resistance to change.

Over the years, lessons have been learned about change processes and reform initiatives in schools. The school leadership team must recognize that change cannot be wholesale and all-encompassing. The change process should unfold in an evolutionary and incremental fashion and contribute to sustained, effective school reform. Leadership for reform to improve student achievement should incorporate strategies that focus on standards and curriculum, specific improvement targets, data-driven instruction, and regular assessment. Any roadblocks that do not allow you to examine and improve processes in these areas must be overcome.

SBM staff members are trained to surmount barricades to school reform. As part of their professional development, they have learned how to find the special attributes that enhance their work. They know that change should be data driven. Accurate data provide for the validation of instructional decisions. Data allow SBM staff members to longitudinally track growth in student achievement.

Trained school professionals also know how to plow through the blockades that hold back change processes and personal empowerment. They have developed the ability to break through the constraints associated with bureaucracy, conflict, and the lack of time to complete all of their tasks (Spreitzer & Quinn, 1996).

For example, change can be blocked when school bureaucracy is consumed by short-term thinking, lack of vision, and infinite layers of administration and reporting. In this resistive situation, initiative for improved inputs is seen to flow exclusively from the top down. Administrators discourage or undervalue the abilities of subordinates.

Another barrier to positive change is conflict between departments in the school system or among peers in the school. Mustering support for change is tenuous at best if administrators are vying for control of programs and resources, or if teachers are competing for a coveted position in the school.

On top of these aggravating situations, there may be intense constraints affecting time to do your job right. This could lead to a stressful school climate. Staff members may report that they lack adequate time even for their current functions, which makes it impossible for them to develop plans for productive improvement.

In overcoming barriers to the implementation of worthwhile change, site administrators and teachers must be able to objectively assess both their work and their roles in the school. This is accomplished when professional development objectives such as those outlined in the previous chapter have been implemented to empower staff to take leadership responsibilities.

A large part of managing change is having school leaders develop the skills to understand individual reactions to change. Therefore, schools need leaders who can help staff members find their true potential. This requires buy-in from a majority of those participating in the change process. To accomplish this task, school leaders should master the skills that advance change processes in interacting, developing, encouraging, and actuating (IDEA) positive reform. The school leadership team needs to get the big IDEA, when it:

Interacts

- Communicates clearly and honestly.
- Listens intently and promotes two-way discussion.
- Understands verbal and nonverbal communication.
- Identifies and overcomes negativity.
- Treats objections and conflict constructively.
- Handles difficult situations with tactful skill.
- Asks the right questions at the right time.

Develops

- Unlocks the potential of others.
- Promotes personal responsibility for individual development.
- Knows when direction is appropriate and when it's not.
- Realizes the needs of staff members as learners.
- Accommodates different learning styles.
- Advocates skills acquisition along with knowledge accumulation.

Encourages

- Employs strategies that motivate and empower.
- Affords useful input in a nonjudgmental way.
- Instills commitment through positive change processes.

- Gives feedback that improves attitude and instruction.
- Recognizes and rewards success.

Actuates

- Establishes a learning culture focused on student achievement.
- Appreciates the practical application of educational theories.
- Incorporates performance standards.
- Sets objectives that ensure performance improvement.
- Uses appropriate measurement indicators.
- Conveys the need for cost-effectiveness.
- Builds a leadership role that makes a difference.

Effective school leaders practice the theory of power investment. Teachers are empowered to make their decisions and actions count, which forges increased self-confidence and leads to new perspectives on what works to improve teaching and learning. And as change processes get under way in the school, each staff member should be encouraged to consider an all-important axiom. Empowerment is not something granted by the central administration; you must empower yourself (Quinn, 1996).

With empowerment, school staff members know how to locate and use their focal points in teaching, learning, and interrelating with colleagues and students, the keystones to high levels of personal performance (Tracy, 2003). When achievement goals are not accomplished as planned, the leadership team and teachers ask, "What in our school curriculum, instructional program, or school culture is contributing to this difficulty?"

In looking for answers that will move them ahead, the school's staff members do not impede the implementation of tested teaching and learning strategies. As problems are identified, trained school personnel do not place the blame on circumstances beyond their control. Instead, heads-up teachers find ways to circumvent stumbling blocks. They continually advance toward the school's academic objectives.

To overcome possible school and community resistance to change, school leaders adopt a blueprint for success. School planning is adjusted so that staff members can align and realign resources to improve student achievement outcomes. Classroom instruction, support services, and school partnerships such as those discussed in chapter 5 focus on areas of learning where students will reap the greatest reward for the investment of time and resources. School resources are removed from those areas that do not effectively impact improvements in student learning or socialization, and those resources are applied to teaching and learning interventions that produce measurable results.

Performance might be measured in terms of improved academic outcomes for students, levels of student motivation and behavior, and the degree of staff and student collegiality demonstrated in an uplifted school culture. Accurate measurements of the change process afford a clear focus on curriculum priorities and provide relevant data for a graphic picture of the direction in which your school is moving. As discussed in chapter 2, use these measurements to adjust your school improvement plan and heighten its quality and effectiveness.

Schools that accomplish efficient game plans, those that find their true potential in the face of instability in the community or discord in the school district, are the ones that become the blue-ribbon schools and win the gold stars. Schools with staff members who cannot perform workable strategic analyses and who fail to provide timely responses to problems will remain static or fall behind in student achievement. These schools could possibly bring upon themselves the loss of accreditation, a real reason to sing the blues.

GETTING STARTED

No school can tackle achievement challenges if its staff members do not open the door and begin the journey that leads to positive change. As Plato put it more than two millennia ago, starting out, envisioning beginning anew, is the most crucial part of our work. Starting a change effort to improve school culture does not guarantee success. However, there is a sure guarantee for failure, and that is not starting. The first obstacle to overcome is simply rising up and getting under way, overcoming collective resistance to action.

It's up to the SBM leadership team to recognize the challenge of staff resistance as essentially a part of human nature, not necessarily the hostility of an obstinate staff, although there may be a few curmudgeons on board. Niccolo Machiavelli's advice to princes in the early 1500s surely overemphasized the role of fear in leadership, but Machiavelli got it right when he asserted that there is nothing harder than taking the lead in introducing a new direction for others to follow. The writings of Machiavelli, like the philosophy of Plato, could as easily be applied to the conditions of educational inertia that exist in many schools today.

Now you may be asking, what is needed to surmount the inertia in my school and begin to unlock the potential of staff members and students? The laws of physics tell us that inertia is overcome with the application of force. In our case, however, "force" is the energy and creativity of the SBM team to do something that begins the change process in restructuring and aligning resources to meet student needs. When effective change is under way, many resources are at the disposal of the school to improve student achievement, but the act of beginning the change process has to be initiated within the school.

Successful teachers and administrators, like successful students, understand change processes. They know the significance and value of their ability to learn, apply new ideas, and expand their knowledge base. They work daily to develop and sustain relevant skills that are current with the demands of their society and economy. For example, technology-linked learning, computer-assisted instruction, and independent research skills are critical elements in today's marketplace and cannot be ignored or underutilized by the school's instructional staff. The school must think in terms of providing students with a competitive advantage to achieve success, an edge either in the pursuit of postsecondary education or a boost in entering into the highly competitive global workforce.

To achieve success, it's imperative for school leaders to see to it that positive change occurs within two interrelated dimensions. That is, the innovations and reforms must take hold at both the school level and the classroom level. Change mandated at the district level that minimally influences the school and rarely reaches the classroom may be good window dressing or media glitz, but it's relatively worthless for improving student achievement.

Schools are fraught with challenges, so useful change must be built on a series of manageable steps. A starting point can usually be identified by the principal or leadership team even in the most conventional, set-in-its-ways environment. Each step in the change process provides short-term essentials, allowing change to ease its way into the day-to-day workings of the school. Change processes gradually overcome inertia and accommodate anticipated requirements for future improvements. Old-guard values and beliefs give way to the adoption of a new school culture.

DISCOVERING UNIQUE TALENTS

Every school is composed of employees who bring an assortment of differences to the educational table. Effective and efficient school organization reconciles these differences and then takes another important step. School leaders identify unique talents among staff members so that they can capitalize on their differences.

For SBM leadership teams to unlock their true potential, they must become skilled in planning that will increase academic returns on the energies and resources invested in professional development and student learning in their schools. This requires more than the amelioration of staff resistance. There must be willingness by school staff members to look introspectively for inherent abilities that will better serve the needs of the school and its students.

Each of us has abilities that make us unique, different from others with whom we work. Our combination of education, skills, experience, and knowledge helps us fashion an area of expertise. In the successful school, administrators and teachers are assigned and developed so that their individual talents are built into strengths that foster and temper the school mission. But how do you go about identifying the strengths of the people in your school?

Scores of programs for developing employee talents and improving organization productivity are available from private entrepreneurs, consultants associated with universities, and a variety of business enterprises. One of these programs could be adopted by the school leadership team or used by the whole school staff to improve overall performance. As we learned in chapter 3, educators profit from concepts advanced in the business sector when those ideas are appropriately meshed with the goals of the school and aligned with the learning needs of school administrators and teachers.

Generally, accelerated learning is premised on the belief that people excel more quickly when they focus on their strengths than when they dwell on weaknesses. Nevertheless, more than a few professional development endeavors, including those in education, address the notion of rectifying deficiencies. However, some staff development programs take a different approach. The Gallup Organization, for example, has developed and tested a program that helps individuals identify their talents and make the best use of them (Buckingham & Clifton, 2001).

The Gallup program is directed at identifying individual talents and turning them into strengths. The program combines textual and Internet formats to help uncover dominant individual talents through a "StrengthsFinder" profile. Program participants can learn their strengths and apply them at work. Once this is accomplished, the strengths of each staff member in the school could be focused on restructuring and aligning resources toward improved academic achievement.

Gallup has placed some focus on the performance of the school principal. One of the Gallup programs delivers a briefing session for high-level school district administrators. It shares research on the principalship, concepts about developing management theories, and planning for succession. What constitutes an effective principal and what goes into the culture of a "strengths-based" school are at the crux of the Gallup approach. Among offerings, the firm also provides a principal leadership series. The series informs participants about ways to use strengths to improve school leadership, more fully engage staff members, and better impact student growth (Gallup Education Division, 2003).

As many training programs reveal, the weight of bringing positive change most often rides on the shoulders of the principal and the school leadership team. School leaders need to be sensitive to the issues that can undermine school-level factors that impact achievement. School staff members need formal training and support in the overall transformation that is sought. They need guidance and follow-up on redefined organizational roles, new patterns of action, and instructional innovations. In short, they need answers. How will the processes of empowerment and reform affect them and impact student achievement?

DOING WHAT IT TAKES

After the strengths of school staff members are determined, the SBM leadership team should turn these assets into schoolwide performance that produces results. Performance can be viewed as a collective journey of school administrators, grade-level or subject-area teacher teams, students, parents, and other active, results-oriented groups working in the school. When everyone is tuned to the same wavelength, they're like a laser beam focused on attaining higher levels of responsibility and performance.

School leaders and instructional staff learn from taking risks and demonstrating new concepts. This occurs when school staff members move beyond the typical isolation and avoidance tendencies that sometimes exist in schools. Changing from isolation to full engagement and collaboration is accomplished more readily when all staff members understand their personal strengths. (See figure 7.1.)

In mastering and using personal strengths, you will likely develop an area of excellence, something that makes you stand out among the school's administrative or instructional staff. Your ability to find and focus on this educational skill, and to effectively share it, can be part of the foundation of your school's success in raising levels of achievement. With a distinct teaching and learning advantage, based on your strong points and competencies, you can help design and put into action the school improvement plan. You can assist in school transformation efforts that will impact student achievement by focusing on the most important school-level factors.

For the past 30 years, research on school effectiveness has identified school-level factors that affect levels of achievement. In his most recent work, Robert Marzano (2003) examined many studies, then prioritized teacher-level, student-level, and school-level factors that influence academic outcomes. In the school-level domain, Marzano collapsed and rank-ordered five factors that affect achievement: (1) a sure and workable curriculum; (2) challenging goals and useful feedback; (3) parent and community involvement; (4) a safe and orderly learning environment; and (5) school staff collegiality and professionalism.

While school leadership is not listed among Marzano's school-level factors, he believes that leadership is critical to positive school change.

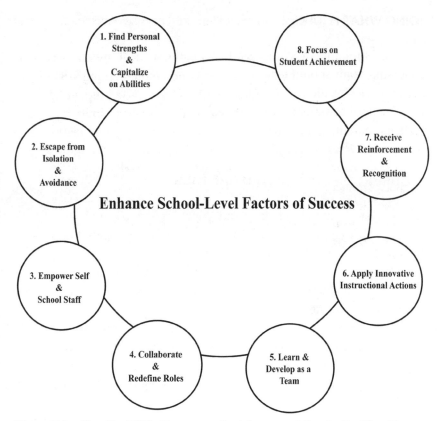

Figure 7.1. The Big IDEA: Overcome Resistance and Create Positive Change, Stepping Stones for School Leaders

Indeed, Marzano says leadership represents an "overarching variable" that influences all school factors.

Maybe you're saying there's nothing astoundingly new in the five school-level factors. However, Marzano singled out the most important ingredient in the mix contributing to student achievement. The really significant element is an "opportunity to learn," adequate content coverage and engaged student enterprise.

Change can be brought to bear on any and all of the five school-level factors, says Marzano, using available resources. Additional assets are not required. This is correct if your resources are adequate. But are the resources in public education ever fully adequate? I would add that the mission of the SBM team and school leaders is to further enhance learning by securing added fiscal inputs to meet identified needs connected to student achievement.

At the school level, the personal strengths of staff members provide advantages beyond teaching, learning, and implementing school improvements. Efforts to transform a school and raise student achievement often require additional financial resources in support of new ideas that heighten abilities in leadership, instruction, and learning.

FOCUSING ON SPECIALIZED ABILITIES

School systems should identify and select leaders on the basis of ability. The SBM leadership team should choose the right people and place them in slots where they can achieve the greatest success for the school. When all school personnel have the best fit, administrators and teachers will better know and appreciate their talents. They'll be able to build on their strengths.

There are keys to the strategic development of strengths that SBM leaders cannot ignore. One key involves specialization. No person can be the end-all and do-all in every matter of school administration or classroom instruction. No one is the personification of all things to all people.

Success in your specialty field is embedded in choices. First, you focus on a particular field in teaching or administration and then you become fully competent in that field so that you can do an excellent job. To come to grips with your true specialization and better meet the needs of your school, there are certain questions that you might ask yourself. What assignments are most motivating and enjoyable for me? Are there tasks in the school that seem hard for others but that I accomplish easily? How can I maximize my contributions to the school? How can I help my colleagues reach their full potential?

To establish a more enlightened focus on your specialization, you must take some time for self-examination. You may already be capitalizing on your strengths, but it doesn't hurt to analyze your accomplishments to reassess your powerful points. Your strongest skills may be those best suited for contributing to the change processes initiated in your school. This is part and parcel to expanding your personal horizons so that your goals align with the school mission. Through professional development and other venues of learning, school staff members should regularly reexamine their strengths, and thus anticipate personal growth hand-in-hand with school improvement.

It goes without saying that when you use your strengths effectively, joy in your work should join with concentration on delivering outstanding performance. School administrators lead better and teachers teach better if they're doing what brings them satisfaction. If helping students to succeed is rewarding and joyful, you'll work all the harder to improve your skills and accomplish the school mission.

We know that successful professionals utilize general skills and also have one or two specialty fields where their performance is consistently noteworthy. It's the job of the school leadership team to direct these staff strengths and the accompanying support where they will produce the most gain. For example, you don't respond to declining scores in mathematics by securing a grant for history teachers to learn how to implement strategies using primary source materials. You've got to pinpoint people and resources where they'll best serve student needs.

Finally, don't postpone initiating change processes until unanimous support develops. You can't lose time waiting for all stakeholders to come on board. Some staff members will never buy into improvements. The leadership team will know when it's time to begin. Improvements should start when consensus has been established among teachers, participating parents, and concerned community members. In the Disney film where Fess Parker plays American hero Davy Crockett, the "King of the Wild Frontier" says: "Be sure you're right, then go ahead."

CHAPTER 7 SUMMARY

Meaningful change overcomes resistance in a series of manageable steps. Successful change won't occur overnight. It's evolutionary and produces sustained, effective school reform. The principal and leadership team understand this and use strategies that address standards and curriculum, targets for improvement, data-driven instruction, and regular assessment. School leaders get the big IDEA; they Interact, Develop, Encourage, and Actuate for reform.

Each phase in the change process provides essentials that incrementally overcome a school's cultural inertia. Identified needs are met one step at a time for long-term improvement. School leaders ensure that useful innovations and reforms are implemented at both the school level and the classroom level. Outmoded ideas slowly crumble beneath the weight of a superior school culture.

Managing change efficiently requires school leaders who can anticipate individual reactions to change. This takes more than the ability to overcome resistance. Superior leaders help others in the school to discover their true potential. School staff members start to look introspectively for strengths that will serve the needs of the school and its students. All learn from taking risks and demonstrating new concepts.

Numerous programs are available to help school staff members find personal strengths and improve organization productivity. Educators who implement reform can benefit from the concepts found in these programs when the training is joined to the goals and needs of the school. In this scenario, administrators and teachers break free of isolation and avoidance tendencies that may fuel resistance to positive change.

Faculty collaboration occurs more readily when all staff members know and master their personal strengths and special abilities. The principal and the school leadership team direct these strengths and specialties where they will do the greatest good for student achievement.

Finally, school leaders can't waste time waiting for the support of all stakeholders. The SBM team will know when it's time to begin the change process, when sufficient consensus has been established among teachers, parents, and members of the community.

CHAPTER 7 REFLECTION AND DISCUSSION

1. What are examples of resistance to change that could lead to problems in bringing reform into a school? What types of resistance have you encountered in your school system?
2. What are some critical steps that can be taken to overcome a school's cultural inertia to change?

3. What can a school leadership team do to unlock the potential of its staff members?

4. Explain how and where positive school change must occur to be truly effective.

5. What school-level factors need to be addressed to improve student achievement? How might overcoming resistance and developing potential enhance efforts to improve school-level factors?

6. How can the unique talents and specialized abilities among school staff members be used to the advantage of implementing school reform?

7. What are the basic elements that come into play when the SBM team gets the "big IDEA"?

CHAPTER 8

Putting It All Together

Very early in his career, Steve McQueen, one of my favorite film stars, played the role of a young football hero gone astray in *The Great St. Louis Bank Robbery* (1959), which was filmed on location and based on an actual heist. McQueen, who had roots in Missouri, drives the getaway car in this quasi-documentary drama. He seems more at home in the movie and performs more admirably than most of the cast, which included local policemen and customers who were in the bank at the time of the actual 1953 shoot-out. In the movie, the team of hoods spends an inordinate amount of time planning every detail of the robbery, yet they never really come to trust one another. Once they are inside the bank, everything that can go wrong does go wrong. Unable to hold together, the St. Louis gang reverts to self-centered survival tactics and scurries to save their own hides.

If your SBM team can't get it together, if they can't effectively actuate a plan with the school and its community, conditions will snap back to where they were, and school-based reform won't be able to get a foothold. Indeed, individual apprehension and school resistance may heighten in response to the failure, making efforts at positive change all the more difficult the next time around. This is why executing your school improvement plan correctly is as critical as the plan itself.

A well-thought-out improvement plan needs a coherent, trusting team behind it, leaders who can adjust on the fly and develop effective contingencies to meet unexpected problems. Moreover, school leaders should have some historical perspective on the past performance of their school—an appreciation for earlier successes and failures, and a full understanding of the terrain that staff members and students have traversed.

On any journey, it's useful to recall the territory we've covered as well as to prepare a roadmap for the territory ahead. Remembering allows us to reassess what we've seen and done, to examine activities helpful as well as episodes botched or just uneventful. At any rate, it's always advisable to file memories for future reference.

The information assembled in the previous chapters covers considerable ground. Like Dorothy and her supportive compatriots in the Land of Oz, we've reached an end point where we might ask ourselves, "What have we learned?" Dorothy forthrightly answered, "There's no place like home." We could respond with equal veracity, "There's no place like our school." Let's take stock, then, of some of the ideas that we've encountered that may help meet the unique needs of our school, basics to contemplate as we take steps to restructure and align resources toward academic success.

STUDYING THE ISSUES

If you've decided to pursue a program to implement SBM in your school, or if you already have a SBM leadership team and wish to sharpen its effectiveness, the place to start is a collective review of the current research. You can't plan and accomplish improvements in isolation, so, as a school team, select topics for in-depth study.

Don't forget to avail yourself of the highly effective research assistance that can be provided by the school librarian. The school library might serve as a hub for after-school research and planning meetings. Possibly the school librarian could direct an on-site clearinghouse of SBM information.

Share up-to-date, relevant information. Flesh out those concepts reviewed in this text that you consider most essential. Align important SBM features with the particular needs that your team identifies in your school. Go through this procedure on a regular basis. But remember the gang in *The Great St. Louis Bank Robbery*. Perfect planning and rehearsal can go awry during execution if sufficient trust is lacking among team members or if the team has no faith in its leadership.

As you build trusting relationships around a research-based model, fiscal management at the school site will call for the comprehensive training of staff members. Ongoing support of all elements of the school must come from the leadership team. Some degree of on-site budgetary control is highly important, but additional factors need to be in place. Managerial know-how, sharing reliable information, and procedures for the recognition of school staff for their accomplishments are part of the SBM framework. Paramount to restructuring and aligning resources, however, is that your goal stay soundly fixed on improving student achievement.

Aligning the school's resources for faculty and student successes works best when school staff members display entrepreneurial skills, creativity, and self-reliance. School staff can learn how to circumvent bureaucratic roadblocks, discover resources that help students learn, and instill results-oriented instruction across subject areas and grade levels. School leaders need to be able to proficiently adapt to change, take risks to create opportunities, and quickly secure appropriate resources when they become available.

Meaningful restructuring and alignment are achieved when the school manifests flexible operations that are data driven and needs based. Needs are determined regularly using school performance reviews that diagnose student strengths and weaknesses, recognize instructional difficulties, and introduce effective interventions designed to improve student achievement.

Above all, communication between the district's central administration and the school leadership team must be clear-cut and explicit. Dialogue should flow freely, and the interchange of ideas should manifest shared educational convictions.

CONTROLLING THE PURSE STRINGS

When site-based management and site-based budgeting come together as a school's operational model, the selection should be the choice of the staff members at the school site. Site-based budgeting calls for a strong and sustained commitment from the school and its community. Little or nothing is accomplished when SBM is externally mandated and left to bud and blossom unattended, without funds set aside that nurture adequate training and follow-up support.

In a SBM environment, financial planning encompasses more than managing appropriations and expenditures. Overseeing finances goes far beyond the mere acceptance of a fixed budget at face value. Fiscal management must account for the concerns of the whole school community. This requires school data that originate in annual, reliable needs assessments. Budgetary decision making is grounded in data that delineate faculty, student, parent, and communitywide exigencies.

It's critical that the school budget be tied to the annual needs assessment and the school improvement plan. When connected and aligned, these three sources of information allow for superior problem solving, because the school leadership team will have a complete picture of the school at its disposal as it designs strategies to uplift academic outcomes.

Strategies to overcome deficiencies are put into operation within the framework of practical school actions implemented by teachers and students in the classrooms. These frontline actions are supported by families, concerned citizens, and businesses in the school community. Raising student achievement depends on the collective alignment of needs, goals, and the wise application of school resources.

In schools where the SBM team can operate within a high-involvement budgetary system, staff recruitment and expenses, utility costs, the source of services and supplies, and carryover of unspent monies are controlled at the school level. It's more likely, however, that on-site budgetary control will be limited to authority over discretionary monies. The application of discretionary school funds can and should be supplemented by outside resources acquired through fundraising activities, grants, and partnerships, but always targeted toward a cohesive instructional program.

To monitor school finances, one of the following budgetary approaches, or a combination of them, is usually used: (1) line-item budgeting; (2) performance budgeting; (3) program-planning budgeting; (4) zero-based budgeting; or (5) outcome budgeting. Regardless of the approach, a cash management policy that follows set procedures must be in place to precisely account for all incoming and outgoing funds.

The form that leadership takes in the school ultimately determines those who have control of the school's purse strings. Site-based budgeting may be democratic, principal led, or council directed. Whatever the process, consensus is crucial. Achieving schoolwide consistency calls for the principal's direct or shared responsibility for all fiscal matters.

SHOOTING FOR SCHOOL-BASED COHERENCE

Taking into account the plethora of business and management responsibilities in the school, principals spend lots of time on issues other than instruction. Every year, noninstructional responsibilities seem to grow, lessening the amount of time available for classroom visits, professional development, or student academic needs. And dealing with managerial chores, including those of a fiscal nature, can seriously hinder the creation of a coherent instructional program. Therefore, school leaders must learn to budget time as well as money where it will do the most good.

"Shoot for the stars," principals tell their students. Principals can do the same. Practical steps can be taken to plant and stimulate the growth of an instructional program that produces coherence. Principals promote program coherence when they serve the school as consultative instructional leaders who guide teacher development, and as leaders of learning who acquire innovative skills to enhance school climate and culture. In short, everyone in the school community benefits when the principal and SBM leaders model the importance of lifelong learning.

Constructive leadership techniques can be drawn from the world of business as well as education. Complementary concepts from both fields come together to define effective school-based practices. As a first step, leadership should eliminate fear. Good school leaders promote openness, sharing, and professional freedom within the context of accountability.

The SBM leadership team learns from mistakes and never accepts failure. Outstanding school leaders continually organize and reorganize the resources of the school in such a way as to increase the successes of both students and faculty. Heading up the SBM leadership team, the principal is a skillful strategic planner who achieves consensus on the school mission, establishes an instructionally coherent program to meet the learning needs of all students, and uses consultative communication to assist teachers, students, and parents.

A consultative approach to leadership can put your school on the path to success and increase the academic returns on your instructional investment. The principal and the SBM team, working together, can amplify levels of personal performance by using a consensus-building, facilitative leadership style. First, listen open-mindedly to the concerns of all. Then develop well-thought-out, collaborative solutions to problems. Finally, emphasize the school mission as a selling point on which to build communitywide support. Consultative leadership may serve to strengthen instructional coherence, improve learning outcomes, counter the achievement gap, and help school staff members and students more ably meet state standards.

REELING IN RESOURCES

Seek and ye shall find. Let the community know your school's needs. Design and follow a congruous fundraising plan. Cast a wide net when collecting your assets. Muster extensive support and establish a commitment on the part of the community before setting off on your fundraising endeavors.

The SBM leadership team identifies and acquires the specific resources needed by the school that will benefit teaching and learning. There are many ways to acquire resources, and the school should utilize all of them. Local money-making activities can help meet short-term needs. Long-term developmental funds or grant proposals can be used for larger projects. Pursue assistance from multiple sources. Funding of school programs is most secure when it does not rely on a single strategy.

When you're sure you know your school's needs, research possible funding sources. Prepare grant proposals strictly according to grantor instructions, with readability as a guidepost. Once you've got the grant, regularly evaluate and report on your program to secure renewable support.

A local education foundation (LEF) should be set up by the school district or cooperating school systems. A LEF is the best way to go after big dollar acquisitions. The LEF is more appealing to contributors when it has a nonprofit 501(c)(3) tax status for donor tax write-offs. If your district doesn't have a LEF, start one.

Compromise is the key to uncovering suitable resources that originate from dissimilar, perhaps conflicting constituencies. The SBM team that assembles multiple and diverse funding packages directs all resources toward a coherent instructional focus. This practice spawns stability in the school program. School leaders must be diligent so as not to diffuse funds among unconnected supports. A coherent instructional framework gets first consideration in seeking and appropriating resources.

Agreement among staff members on the school mission, that is, a trusting, collegial relationship and a common agenda, is essential to finding resources and applying them where they will get the most bang for the buck. Ultimately, those in control of the school's finances are also the most accountable for academic results. Abundant resources that accomplish little in the way of improved student performance cannot be justified.

LINKING WITH THE COMMUNITY

School partnerships with businesses and community organizations can provide a variety of programs that enhance the quality of education. Arts, cultural, and scientific institutions in your school's community should be approached to create educational partnerships that improve student motivation and interest in learning, and that broaden understanding of career options for participants.

Often partnerships with community institutions can bring students of diverse cultures and backgrounds together in cooperative learning teams. These activities can positively impact student socialization as students help one another to achieve common goals. Moreover, experiential learning beyond the classroom provides students with concrete tasks that reinforce intellectual curiosity and academic knowledge.

Partnership programs can serve as advocates of community literacy, appreciation of the arts, and scientific inquiry. For example, activities might focus on creative thinking, cultural diversity, the shared heritage of the community, applications of technology, or environmental awareness. A partnership program that provides exposure to a fuller repertoire of ways to learn will improve student abilities to acquire and analyze useful information in school and throughout life.

Public institutions in urban and rural areas around the country readily assist the schools in their communities. School partnerships can be highly productive when resources are coordinated among several sponsoring institutions and when the activities enhance school curricula and state educational standards. Partnerships should promote a learning culture of collaboration and self-evaluation where both parties benefit from the association and work together toward program improvement.

School staff members and partnership representatives need to fit program activities into the school mission. As your school restructures resources to elevate academic outcomes, the SBM leadership team should align the broadening experiences of partnerships with your school's learner-centered program. Procedures should be in place to train teachers and partnership volunteers to capitalize on the student learning activities.

DESIGNING PRACTICAL STAFF DEVELOPMENT

Appropriate professional development is vital if you expect to see successful school-based practices put into action. Targeted professional development should include training in SBM fiscal matters, leadership styles, change processes, and proven innovations in teaching and learning. Without proper training, school leaders will be less capable of securing and allocating resources where they'll do the greatest good for students. Staff exposure to leadership skills can include training that employs role playing, case studies, and experiential activities meshed with the unique needs of the school.

Cohesive leadership in the school pivots on the principal. But the needs of schools cannot be met by "cookie-cutter principals" using standardized leadership tactics. The best training of school leaders is customized to the circumstances in the school. And in all cases, good leaders must learn how to grapple with hard issues that appear beyond solution. In this respect, one perspective helpful to investigating and assessing school leadership styles is found in Michael Fullan's five ingredients for improvement: moral purpose, understanding change, relationship building, knowledge sharing, and coherence making.

Practical, targeted staff development positively affects student achievement when it's explicitly connected to the instructional program. Training should address the needs of heterogeneous student populations, classroom assessment, and team collaboration. Some training of teachers should occur on the job. Teacher professional development in the school classroom that is inquiry based and linked to expected student outcomes is usually superior to seminars or activities conducted away from the school.

If staff development is on target, the school culture will elevate faculty professionalism. Student learning improves when teachers are knowledgeable in their subjects, use strategies that motivate learners, and exchange ideas that work in their school. When instructional staff members train as teams, achievement outcomes gain ground.

School leaders and professional development consultants should confer beforehand with those who will receive training. Often teachers who are pursuing new concepts can assist in planning the type of training that will be best suited to reaching their objectives.

Teachers and administrators should evaluate their learning experiences to determine if they've achieved sought-after objectives. The extent to which professional development has become institutionalized in your school should be measured with surveys, interviews, and observations of classroom instruction. This helps to determine the quality of staff training.

Trends in improved student achievement should become apparent over time if adequate training and effective implementation of the professional development have occurred. Evaluation of training at the school level is critical. You need to know if your staff development program is accomplishing the results it was designed to achieve.

DISCOVERING POTENTIAL

Practical staff development can unlock hidden potential, cash in on individual strengths, and produce staff collegiality and cohesiveness in the school. Professional training and on-site action research can be part of the managed steps that help school leaders overcome resistance to worthwhile change.

Leaders must recognize that sustainable school revitalization is an evolutionary process. In this respect, the principal and SBM team anticipate reactions to change and use strategies that incrementally chip away at resistance. The school faculty is encouraged to come out of classroom isolation, work in teams that initiate elements of positive change, and see reform translated into student successes. The school's cultural inertia to change is surmounted when school leaders get the big IDEA; they Interact, Develop, Encourage, and Actuate for school reform.

To be effective, administrative reforms and instructional innovations must take hold at both the school and classroom levels. This takes a leadership team with willingness to help all parties in the school discover their true potential. Strengths are identified and utilized to best serve the needs of the school and its students.

Many programs exist that school leaders might access for staff members to determine their personal strengths and improve performance. Selected training that uncovers the latent talents of school staff members and capitalizes on their specialized abilities bolsters staff collegiality and should be tied to the school mission.

When strengths and specialties are determined, school leaders should focus these skills where they will most effectively impact student achievement. But school leaders can't wait around hoping for 100% staff buy-in. The SBM team must initiate the change process when general agreement exists among teachers, parents, and the school community that the time has come to improve school operations and student performance.

CONCLUSION

Implementing SBM, site-based budgeting, and the collective leadership required to improve school culture and student achievement is time-consuming and difficult. When it all comes together, it creates a harmonious framework for responding to the unique needs of each school's student population. Specific resources can be acquired to address weak instructional areas, and those resources can be targeted for maximum effect. But the bottom line in procuring and allocating resources is, of course, whether expenditures have improved student achievement. Staff empowerment and on-site budgetary control may result in a resilient school culture, but if they produce little or no effect on learning and standardized test scores, our SBM script hasn't played well. It's unlikely that our production will have a long run.

On the other hand, SBM can breathe new life into a school when it's properly cast, that is, when students and their achievement are spotlighted at center stage. As you acquire and allocate resources, you can't lose sight of your basic goal, to advance student capabilities and successes. As a concerned principal once told me, "The school mission is more important than any one person or program."

CHAPTER 8 REFLECTION AND DISCUSSION

1. Why is resilient carry-through on the implementation of school improvements as critical as a well-conceived school improvement plan?
2. How might the school library and the services of the librarian benefit the planning and development of a SBM initiative?
3. What are the primary developmental areas to consider and what steps do you take in putting together a sustainable SBM plan?
4. How does the school leadership team achieve the full integration of the annual needs assessment, improvement plan, and school budget? What does this accomplish?
5. How might staff development programs adopted from the world of business be applied to a school? Locate and research such a program and create a plan for integrating it into your school's professional development activities.
6. What aspect of the school program has top priority in the acquisition and disbursement of school funds? Why is this so important to student achievement?
7. Why are ongoing evaluation of programs and internal self-assessment critical to the operations and outcomes of the school?

References

The bibliographic resources consulted for this study cover a wide range of materials and subjects. References appear below by chapter number, listed alphabetically under each chapter. For the sake of brevity, a reference to a particular work is cited only once, that is, when the source first contributes to a chapter in the text. Obviously, concepts derived from particular sources may have associations with ideas expressed throughout the book. In no case, however, are direct quotations from other works not specifically credited when they appear in the text.

There are literally hundreds of worthwhile sources related to the topics examined in this text that do not appear in the references below. Indeed, new and pertinent educational research is brought to our attention almost daily. As you conduct your own research to implement school-based practices designed to improve student achievement, you will develop a working bibliography geared to the needs of your school. Your school librarian can be a major player in this effort. The materials cited here, however, may serve as a point of origin from which to begin your progress down the research road.

Many of the references listed below contain World Wide Web addresses that may be accessed on the Internet. In some respects, these references provide one of the most important resources that you may derive from this text. These Internet sites and the research links they contain afford a wealth of information to aid school staff members in all manner of research on school-based management.

PREFACE

Friedman, M., & Friedman, R. (1979). *Free to choose: A personal statement.* New York: Harcourt Brace Jovanovich.

McCullough, D. (2001). *John Adams.* New York: Touchstone Book published by Simon & Schuster. John Adams to Matthew Robinson, March 23, 1786. Adams Papers, Massachusetts Historical Society, Boston, MA.

Toffler, A. (1980). *The third wave.* New York: William Morrow.

CHAPTER 1, FOLLOWING THE RESEARCH ROAD

Alexander, C., Boyer, H., Brownson, A. B., Clark, C., Jennings, J., & Patrick, E. (2000, December). Resource allocation practices and student achievement: An examination of district expenditures by performance level with interviews from twenty-one districts. Southwest Educational Development Laboratory and University of Texas at Austin. OERI, U.S. Dept. of Education. Retrieved January 25, 2003, from http://www.sedl.org/pubs/policy24/

Council of the Great City Schools. ([1996]). Promising practices: A reform effort of the Boston public schools to encourage site-based management and shared decision-making. Retrieved February 1, 2003, from http://www.cgcs.org/promise/whatworks/reform/part17.html

Council of the Great City Schools. (2000a, February). An analysis of state funding of the Baltimore city public schools; (2000b, January) . . . of the New York City public schools; (1998, June) . . . of the Philadelphia public schools. Retrieved January 25, 2003, from http://www.cgcs.org/taskforce/finance3.html

Council of the Great City Schools. (2002a). Finance: Goals of the task force. Urban Education Task Force. Task Force Reports. Raising student achievement in the Dayton public schools. Appendix E. Retrieved January 25, 2003, from http://www.cgcs.org/taskforce/finance3.html

Council of the Great City Schools and Manpower Demonstration Research Corporation. (2002b). *Foundations for success: Case studies of how urban systems improve achievement.* Retrieved January 26, 2003, from http://www.cgcs.org/reports/Abstract/html

Cromwell, S. (2000, June 26). Site-based management: Boon or boondoggle? *Education World.* Retrieved September 15, 2003, from http://www.education-world.com/a_admin/admin176.shtml

Cross City Campaign for Urban School Reform. (2000a). School-based budgeting and school-based management. Retrieved January 26, 2003, from http://www.crosscity.org/programs/budgeting

Cross City Campaign for Urban School Reform. (2000b). Seattle, highlights of school reform. Retrieved January 26, 2003, from http://www.crosscity .org/cities/seattle/highlights.htm

David, J. L. (1995/96, December/January). The who, what, and why of school-based management. *Educational Leadership, 53*(4). Retrieved February 9, 2003, from http://www.ascd.org/readingroom/edlead/9512/david.html

Eggers, W. D. (2002). Show me the money: Budget-cutting strategies for cash-strapped states. Washington, D.C.: American Legislative Exchange Council; and New York City: Manhattan Institute for Policy Research. Retrieved February 1, 2003, from http://www.alec.org/meSWFiles/pdf/ShowMeTheMoney2 .pdf

Goertz, M. E. (2001, March). Comprehensive school reform and school-based budgeting in New Jersey. Paper presented at the 26th annual meeting of the American Education Finance Association, Cincinnati. ED 456 534.

Gleason, S., Donahue, N., & Leader, G. (1995/96, December/January). Boston revisits school-based management. *Educational Leadership, 53*(4).

Hadderman, M. (1999, October). School-based budgeting. ERIC Digest 131. Retrieved January 28, 2003, from http://eric.uoregon.edu/publications/ digests/digest131.html

Hannaway, J. (1993). Decentralization in two school districts: Challenging the standard paradigm. In J. Hannaway & M. Carnoy (eds.), *Decentralization and school improvement: Can we fulfill the promise?* San Francisco: Jossey-Bass.

Holloway, J. H. (2000). The promise and pitfalls of site-based management. *Educational Leadership, 57*(2). Retrieved January 26, 2003, from http:// www.ascd.org/readingroom/edlead/0004/holloway.html

Kedro, M. J. (1993, January 6). Opinion shaper: Education research like "magic bag." *St. Louis Suburban Journals, Southwest County Journal*.

Kedro, M. J. (2003, January). Controlling the purse strings. *Principal Leadership, 3*(5). National Association of Secondary School Principals.

Missouri Department of Elementary and Secondary Education. (2002, January 8). State, St. Louis school district, win major grants to help strengthen school leadership. *News Release, 36*(3). Retrieved February 2, 2003, from http://www.dese.state.mo.us/news/2002/SAELP.html

National Education Association. (1996). Trends: Moving toward school-based management during budget cutbacks. From the 2000–2001 New Member CD. Retrieved February 8, 2003, from http://www.nea.org

New England Comprehensive Assistance Center. (1999). Resources: Links: Site based management. Retrieved February 8, 2003, from http://www.edc.org/ NECAC/resources/links/links-sitebmgmt.html

North Central Regional Educational Laboratory. (1993). Decentralization: Why, how, and toward what ends? Rationale and history of Chicago school reform. Retrieved February 8, 2003, from http://www.ncrel.org/sdrs/areas/issues/envrnmnt/go/93-1hess.htm

Olson, L. (1997, June 4). Power of the purse. *Education Week*. Retrieved February 8, 2003, from http://www.edweek.org/ew/vol-16/36sbb.h16

Peterson, D. (1991). School-based budgeting. ERIC Digest. Eugene, OR: ERIC Clearinghouse on Educational Management, University of Oregon. ED 336 865.

Ryan, S., Bryk, A., Lopez, G., Williams, K., & Luppescu, S. (1997). *Charting reform: LSCs—local leadership at work*. Chicago: Consortium on Chicago School Research (CCSR). See http://www.consortium-chicago.org

St. Louis Public Schools. (1996). St. Louis board of education policy, philosophy, goals and objectives: School-based management, PO110. Retrieved January 25, 2003, from http://www.slps.org/boardofeducation/policies/0110.htm

St. Louis Public Schools. (n.d. [2002]). Board of education vision and mission. Retrieved January 25, 2003, from http://www.slps.org/BoardofEducation/objectiv.html

Stiefel, L., Berne, R., Iatarola, P., & Fruchter, N. (2000, Spring). High school size: Effects on budgets and performance in New York City. *Educational Evaluation and Policy Analysis, 22*(1).

U.S. General Accounting Office. (1994). Education reform: School-based management results in changes in instruction and budgeting. GAO/HEHS Publication No. 94–135. Washington, D.C.: Government Printing Office.

Wohlstetter, P., & Mohrman, S. A. (1994). School-based management: Promise and process. CPRE Finance Briefs, U.S. Dept. of Education. Retrieved January 26, 2003, from http://www.ed.gov/pubs/CPRE/fb5sbm.html

Wohlstetter, P., & Van Kirk, A. (1995, April). School-based budgeting: Organizing for high performance. Paper presented at the annual American Educational Research Association Conference, San Francisco. ED 384 953.

Wong, K. K. (2003, Winter). The big stick. *Education Next, 3*(1). Retrieved July 24, 2003, from http://www.educationnext.org/20031/44.html

CHAPTER 2, SCHOOL-BASED FINANCIAL PLANNING

Ackman, D. (ed.). (2002, November 6). Nobel laureate debunks economic theory. Retrieved February 28, 2003, from http://www.forbes.com/home/2002/11/06/cx_da_1106nobel1.html

Apple, M. W., & Beane, J. A. (eds.). (1995). *Democratic schools*. Alexandria, VA: Association for Supervision and Curriculum Development.

Ballou, D. (1996). The condition of urban school finance: Efficient resource allocation in urban schools. National Center for Education Statistics, *Selected papers in school finance 1996*. Retrieved February 22, 2003, from http://www.nces.ed.gov/pubs98/finance/98217-4.html

Candoli, I. C., Hack, W. G., & Ray, J. R. (1998). *School business administration: A planning approach* (6th ed.). Boston: Allyn & Bacon.

Community Education Centers, SLPS. (2002). Office of community education. Retrieved February 22, 2003 from http://locations.slps.org/location .cfm?RecordID=827&BGCOLOR=white

Cooley, W., & Bickel, W. (1986). *Decision-oriented educational research*. Boston: Kluwer-Nijhoff.

Guthrie, J. W. (1996). Reinventing education finance: Efficient resource allocation in urban schools. National Center for Education Statistics, *Selected papers in school finance 1996*. Retrieved April 9, 2003, from http://www .nces.ed.gov/pubs98/finance/98217-5.html

Halaska, C. (n.d.). Social design. Budget builder analysis. [Budget Builder Web Site, Seattle Public School District.] Retrieved March 9, 2003, from http://www.socialdesign.org/bbanalysis/dissdesc.html

Hall, G. (2002, May). Principal connections. *After School Issues, 2*(3), 3–4. National Institute on Out-of-School Time. Cross-Cities Network for Leaders of Citywide After-School Initiatives. Retrieved February 17, 2003, from http://www.wellesley.edu/WCW/CRW/SAC/cross_cities_brief7.pdf

Hutchins, C. L. (1996). *Systemic thinking: Solving complex problems*. Aurora, CO: Professional Development Systems. Retrieved February 17, 2003, see http://www.personal.psu.edu/staff/s/m/smc258/KB/Hutchins.htm

Kahneman, D., & Tversky, A. (1982). *Judgment under uncertainty: Heuristics and biases*. Cambridge, UK: Cambridge University Press.

Maryland State Department of Education. (n.d.). Developing your school improvement plan. Retrieved March 29, 2003, from http://www.mdk12.org/ process/developing/

Murphy, K. (2003, February 21). New student commons building made possible by $1 million gift. *[St. Louis] South County Times*.

Myers, D., & Stonehill, R. (1993). School-based management: OER consumer guide number 4. Retrieved February 23, 2003, from http://www.ed.gov/pubs/ OR/ConsumerGuides/baseman.html

New Jersey Department of Education. (2002). Whole school reform school-based budget: Three-year operational plan / one-year school-based budget. Retrieved April 4, 2003, from http://www.nj.gov/njded/abbotts/sbb/op_plan.htm

Odden, A., Archibald, S., & Tychsen A. (1999, August). Farnham elementary school: A case study of resource reallocation. Resource Reallocation Studies. Consortium for Policy Research in Education (CPRE), University of

Wisconsin–Madison. Retrieved March 1, 2003, from http://www.wcer.wisc .edu/cpre/finance/related/studies/reallocation.asp

Osborne, D., & Gaebler, T. (1992). *Reinventing government: How the entrepreneurial spirit is transforming the public sector*. Reading, MA: Addison-Wesley.

Rhode Island Department of Elementary and Secondary Education. (1999–2003). Writing a school improvement plan. Retrieved March 29, 2003, from http://www.ridoe.net/schoolimprove/salt/guides/sip_writ.htm

Rochester, J. M. (2002). *Class warfare: Besieged schools, bewildered parents, betrayed kids, and the attack on excellence*. San Francisco: Encounter Books.

Rowland, M. (2003, February). Behavioral finance. *Something Better, 30*(4). Missouri National Education Association.

Schomker, M. (1999). *Results: The key to continuous school improvement* (2nd ed.). Alexandria, VA: Association for Supervision and Curriculum Development.

School Redesign Network. (n.d. [2003]). Stanford University. Retrieved April 5, 2003, from http://www.stanford.edu/dept/SUSE/csrn/index.html

Sweeny, B. (1997). A recommended process for analyzing a school improvement plan. Resources for Staff and Organization Development, Wheaton, IL. Retrieved March 30, 2003, from http://www.teachermentors.com/ RSOD%20Site/SIP/AnalyzeSIPcolor.html

Texas Education Agency. (2002, September). Financial accountability system resource guide update 9.0. Retrieved March 1, 2003, from http://www .tea.state.tx.us/school.finance/audit/rewsguide9/sbdm/

Thompson, D. C., & Wood, R. C. (2001). *Money and schools: A handbook for practitioners* (2nd ed.). Larchmont, NY: Eye on Education.

U.S. Dept. of Education. (1998, October). *Implementing schoolwide programs— An idea book on planning*. Section 3, Planning schoolwide program change. Step 2: Conducting a comprehensive needs assessment. Retrieved February 19, 2003, from http://www.ed.gov/pubs/Idea_Planning/Step_2.html

Wagman, J. (2003, February 12). Audits detail problems in school finances. *St. Louis Post-Dispatch*.

Wohlstetter, P., & Mohrman, S. A. (1996). *Assessment of school-based management*. USC and OERI, U.S. Dept. of Education. Retrieved February 15, 2003, from http://www.ed.gov/pubs/SER/SchBasedMgmt/ The above-referenced site synthesizes work in the field, including (a) Hentschke, G. (1988). Budgetary theory and reality. In *Microlevel school finance*. Cambridge, MA: Ballinger; (b) Lawler, E. E. (1986). *High involvement management*. San Francisco: Jossey-Bass; (c) Lawler, E. E. (1992). *The ultimate advantage: Creating the high involvement organization*. San Francisco: Jossey-Bass.

CHAPTER 3, CONSULTATIVE LEADERSHIP, BUDGETING FOR INSTRUCTIONAL COHERENCE

American Evaluation Association. (2002). Position statement on high stakes testing in pre-K–12 education. Retrieved April 19, 2003, from http://www .eval.org/hst3.htm

American Institutes for Research. (1999). An educator's guide to schoolwide reform. Arlington, VA: Educational Research Service. Retrieved April 19, 2003, from http://www.aasa.org/issues_and_insights/district_organization/ Reform/overview.htm

Bennis, W., & Nanus, B. (1985). *Leaders: The strategies for taking charge.* New York: Harper & Row.

Council of the Great City Schools and Manpower Demonstration Research Corporation. (2002). *Foundations for success: Case studies of how urban school systems improve achievement.* An abstract. Retrieved April 19, 2003, from http://www.cgcs.org/reports/Abstract.html

Deming, W. E. (1986). *Out of the crisis.* Cambridge, MA: MIT Press.

Doyle, M. E., & Rice, D. M. (2002, November). A model for instructional leadership. *Principal Leadership, 3*(3). National Association of Secondary School Principals. Retrieved April 22, 2003, from http://www.nassp.org/ news/pl_model_1102.html

Dreyfuss, G. O., Cistone, P. J., & Divita, C., Jr. (1992). Restructuring in a large district: Dade county, Florida. In Glickman, C. D. (ed.), *Supervision in transition: The 1992 ASCD yearbook.* Alexandria, VA: Association for Supervision and Curriculum Development.

DuFour, R. (2002, May). The learning-centered principal. *Educational Leadership, 59*(8), 12–15. Association for Supervision and Curriculum Development. Retrieved April 22, 2003, from http://www.ascd.org/readingroom/ edlead/0205/dufour.html

Guskey, T. R. (1990, February). Integrating innovations—integrate a collection of models. *Educational Leadership, 47*, 11–15.

Hallinger, P., & Murphy, J. (1985, November). Assessing the instructional management behavior of principals. *Elementary School Journal, 86*, 217–247.

Kedro, M. J. (1990, March). Functions, practices, and classroom models for SLPS instructional coordinators. SLPS Division of Research, Assessment and Evaluation.

Kedro, M. J. (2004, April). Coherency: when the puzzle is complete. A consultative approach to instructional coherency. *Principal Leadership, 4*(8). National Association of Secondary School Principals.

Kedro, M. J., Forde, G., & Short, W. (2000, December). Common instructional practices in elementary schools with two-year consistent MAP improvement.

Division of Research, Assessment and Evaluation, St. Louis Public Schools. Retrieved April 19, 2003, from http://www.mindspring.com/~raleigh1/ MAP.html

Kedro, M. J., Short, W., et al. (2002, May). Third-year schools of opportunity: Instructional reform model implementation and achievement (interim report). Division of Research, Assessment and Evaluation, St. Louis Public Schools. Retrieved April 19, 2003, from http://www.mindspring.com/ ~raleigh1/SchoolsOp.htm

Kouzes, J. M., & Posner, B. Z. (2002). *The leadership challenge* (3rd ed.). San Francisco: Jossey-Bass.

Lashway, L. (1995, May). Can instructional leaders be facilitative leaders? Clearinghouse on Educational Management, University of Oregon, ERIC Digest 98. Retrieved April 14, 2003, from http://eric.uoregon.edu/publications/digests/digest098.html

Lashway, L. (1999). Trends and issues: Role of the school leader. ERIC Clearinghouse on Educational Management, College of Education, University of Oregon. Retrieved April 19, 2003, from http://eric.uoregon.edu/trends_ issues/rolelead/index.html

National Association of Elementary School Principals. (2001). *Leading learning communities: Standards for what principals should know and be able to do.* Alexandria, VA: NAESP. Retrieved April 24, 2003, from http://www.naesp .org/llc.pdf

Newmann, F. M., Smith B., Allensworth E., & Bryk, A. (2001). Instructional program coherence: What it is and why it should guide school improvement policy. *Educational Evaluation and Policy Analysis, 23*, 297–321. Retrieved April 19, 2003, from http://www.consortium-chicago.org/publications/ p0d02.html

Northwest Regional Educational Laboratory. (2001). The catalog of school reform models. Retrieved April 19, 2003, from http://www.nwrel.org/scpd/ catalog/modellist.asp

Russell, J. S., et al. (1986). *Linking the behaviors and activities of secondary school principals to school effectiveness: A focus on effective and ineffective behaviors.* Eugene, OR: CEPM Publications, University of Oregon.

St. Louis Public Schools. (2001). St. Louis public schools accreditation action strategies. Retrieved April 19, 2003, from http://www.slps.org/Acred. Strategies/accred.htm

Sergiovanni, T. J. (1994). *Building community in schools.* San Francisco: Jossey-Bass.

CHAPTER 4, ACQUIRING THE RESOURCES FOR ACADEMIC SUCCESS

Ascher, C. (1996, April). Moving toward school-based management during budget cutbacks. *Trends*. NEA 2000–2001 New Member CD. National Education Association. Retrieved June 1, 2003, from http://www.nea.org

Chaika, G. (2002, June). Fund-raising ideas: Raise money without selling door-to-door. *Education World*. Retrieved May 31, 2003, from http://www.wysiwyg://8/http://www.education-world.com/a_admin/admin105.shtml

Cunningham, C. (2002, April). Engaging the community to support student success. ERIC Clearinghouse on Educational Management, University of Oregon. Digest 157. Retrieved June 15, 2003, from http://eric.uoregon.edu/publications/digests/digest157.html

Danforth Foundation. (2000). Jefferson School, St. Louis, Missouri: A case study for the Pre-Conference Meeting of Foundation Staff Conference on Educational Leadership, Teachers College, Columbia University, New York. Retrieved May 26, 2003, from http://www.orgs.muohio.edu/forum-scp/Jefferson_School.html

Farrace, B. (2003, January). From equity to adequacy: Allen Odden on school funding in the standards era. *Principal Leadership, 3*(5), 25–28. National Association of Secondary School Principals. Retrieved June 15, 2003, from http://www.nassp.org/news/pl_equity_0103.html

Finance Project. (2002). Out-of-school time project: Finding funding. Washington, D.C. Retrieved May 19, 2003, from http://www.financeproject.org/ostfinancing.htm

Guthrie, J. W. (1996). Reinventing education finance: Alternatives for allocating resources to individual schools. *Selected Papers in School Finance 1996*. National Center for Education Statistics. Retrieved April 9, 2003, from http://nces.ed.gov/pubs98/finance/98217-5.html

Hancock County Community Foundation. (2003, January). CAPE: An educational winner! Greenfield, IN. Retrieved June 15, 2003, from http://www.hccf.cc/cape.htm

Kedro, M. J. (1992, July 8). Opinion shaper: Education's "innovations" nothing new. *St. Louis Suburban Journals, Southwest County Journal*.

Kedro, M. J., Short, W. E., & Hartman, P. (2002, September). Jefferson elementary school and the Jeff-Vander-Lou education initiative. SLPS Division of Research, Assessment and Evaluation, St. Louis, MO.

Levenson, S. (2003, January). A bigger piece of the pie. *Principal Leadership, 3*(5), 14–18. Retrieved June 8, 2003, from http://www.principals.org/news/pl_biggerpiece_0103.html

Lindbergh, C. A. (1992). *Autobiography of values, with an introduction by Reeve Lindbergh.* San Diego: Harvest Book, Harcourt.

Lowell, A. K. (1999, August). Rebuilding a neighborhood—inside and out. *Oberlin Alumni Magazine.* Retrieved August 2, 2002, from http://www.landmarkcenter.org

Miles, K. H. (2000). Critical issue: Rethinking the use of educational resources to support higher student achievement. North Central Regional Educational Laboratory. Retrieved May 19, 2003, from http://www.ncrel.org/sdrs/areas/issues/envrnmnt/go/go600.htm

National Child Care Information Center. (2003, May). Grants and grant writing. U.S. Dept. of Health and Human Services. Retrieved May 19, 2003, from http://www.nccic.org/faqs/grantwriting.html

Pelavin Research Institute. (1997, November). Investing in school technology: Strategies to meet the funding challenge. U.S. Dept. of Education, Office of Educational Technology. Retrieved May 22, 2003, from http://www.ed.gov/pubs/techinvest/

St. Louis Commerce Magazine. (2001, December). Rebuilding Jeff-Vander-Lou. Retrieved June 8, 2003, from http://www.stlcommercemagazine.com/archives/december2001/education.html

SchoolGrants Newsletter. (2003, May). Grant opportunities for k–12 schools. Retrieved June 7, 2003, from http://www.schoolgrants.org/newsletter.htm

Solomon, M., & Ferguson, M. V. (1998). How to build local support for comprehensive school reform. *Getting Better by Design Series, 7.* Arlington, VA: New American Schools.

Starr, L. (2003, January). Show me the money: Tips and resources for successful grant writing. *Education World.* Retrieved January 31, 2003, from http://www.education-world.com/a_curr/profdev039.shtml

Texas Education Agency. (2002, September). Financial accountability system resource guide: 2.12.1 preparation of grant program budgets. Retrieved May 17, 2003, from http://www.tea.state.tx.us/school.finance/audit/resguide9/budget/bud-52.html

U.S. Dept. of Education (2003, May). Forecast of funding opportunities under the Department of Education discretionary grant programs for fiscal year (FY) 2003. Retrieved May 19, 2003, from http://www.ed.gov/offices/OCFO/grants/forecast.html

Vashon Compact. (n.d.). The vashon compact library—downloads, news, and links. Retrieved June 8, 2003, from http://www.vashoncompact.org/html/library/html

Ward, A. (1996, June). Looking for funding? Look at an education foundation. Electronic School. National School Boards Association. Retrieved June 8, 2003, from http://www.electronic-school.com/0696f5.html

Whitmer, W., & Robbins, L. B. (2001, August). Finding the funds you need: A guide for grantseekers. Penn State Community and Economic Development, Cooperative Extension. Retrieved June 7, 2003, from http://cedev.aers.psu.edu/grantwriting/

Wright, E. (2003, February). Finding resources to support rural out-of-school time initiatives. Strategy brief 4(1). Finance Project, Washington, D.C. Retrieved May 26, 2003, from http://www.financeprojectinfo.org/ost/

CHAPTER 5, PARTNERING FOR PROGRESS

Alamprese, J. A., & Erlanger, W. J. (1989). *No gift wasted*, 2 volumes. Washington, D.C.: Cosmos Corporation and U.S. Dept. of Education.

Atkin, J. M. (1990, April 11). On "alliances" and science education. *Education Week*, p. 36.

Blank, M. J., & Langford, B. H. (2000, September). Strengthening partnerships: Community school assessment checklist. Finance Project and Coalition for Community Schools. Retrieved July 27, 2003, from http://npin.org/library/2001/n00586/n00586.html

Carnegie Council on Adolescent Development. (1989). *Turning points: Preparing American youth for the 21st century*. New York: Carnegie Corp., Carnegie Council on Adolescent Development.

Center for Science in the Public Interest. (2002, September 25). Corporate-school partnerships good for profits, not kids. Retrieved July 3, 2003, from http://www.cspinet.org/new/200209252.html

Committee for Economic Development. (1985). *Investing in our children: Businesses and the public schools: A statement*. New York: Committee for Economic Development.

Confluence St. Louis Task Force on Public Education and Economic Development. (1989). *Economic progress through public education: A report on workforce readiness*. St. Louis: Confluence St. Louis.

Council for Corporate and School Partnerships. (1989). *Guiding principles for business and school partnerships*. Available from http://www.corpschoolpartners.org

Engeln, J. (2003). About the council for corporate and school partnerships. National Association of Secondary School Principals. Retrieved July 3, 2003, from http://www.nassp.org/schoolimprove/engeln_ccsp.cfm

ERIC Clearinghouse on Educational Management. (n.d.). Policy report: Business partnerships with schools, bibliography. University of Oregon. Retrieved July 21, 2003, from http://eric.uoregon.edu/publications/policy_reports/business_partnerships/bibliography.html

ERIC Clearinghouse on Educational Management. (n.d.). School-business partnerships. University of Oregon. Retrieved July 21, 2003, from http://eric.uoregon.edu/hot_topics/index.html#school_business

Finance Project (2003, February). Tools for out-of-school time and community school initiatives. Finding resources to support rural out-of-school time initiatives: Strategy brief 4(1). Retrieved May 28, 2003, from http://www.financeprojectinfo.org/ost/

FOCUS St. Louis. (2001). Racial equality in the St. Louis region: A community call to action.

Kedro, M. J. (1989, January). An evaluation of the cub scout initiative program ("inner-city cub scout pilot project") in the St. Louis public schools. SLPS Division of Evaluation and Research.

Kedro, M. J. (1989, November). An evaluation of four specialty programs administered through the partnership office under the metropolitan desegregation settlement plan: Missouri Botanical Garden, Missouri Historical Society, United Nations Association, Vaughn Cultural Center. SLPS Division of Evaluation and Research.

Kedro, M. J. (1990, June). An evaluation of four specialty programs administered through the partnership office under the metropolitan desegregation settlement plan: Saint Louis Art Museum, Saint Louis Science Center/Planetarium, Saint Louis Symphony Orchestra, Saint Louis Zoological Park. SLPS Division of Evaluation and Research.

Kiley, J. S. (1989, Fall). On the road to college: Paving the way. *The College Board Review, 153,* 20–25.

Levine, M., & Trachtman, R. (1988). *American business and the public school.* New York: Teachers College Press.

Minneapolis Public Schools. (n.d.). Business and community school partnerships. Retrieved July 3, 2003, from http://www.mpls.k12.mn.us/involvement/business_partnerships.shtml

Northwest Regional Educational Laboratory. (n.d.). *Putting the pieces together: Comprehensive school-linked strategies for children and families.* Chapter 3. Finding and developing resources. Retrieved July 3, 2003, from http://www.wysiwyg://139/http://www.nwrel.org/cfc/frc/ncrel/chap3.htm

Slavin, R. E., & Madden, N. A. (1979, Spring). School practices that improve race relations. *American Educational Research Journal, 16*, 169–180.

U.S. Dept. of Education. (1986). *What works: Schools that work, educating disadvantaged children.* Washington, D.C.: Government Printing Office.

U.S. Dept. of Education. (1987). *What works: Research about teaching and learning* (2nd ed.). Washington, D.C.: Government Printing Office.

Weinstein, C., Ridley, D. S., Dahl, T., & Weber, E. S. (1988/1989, December/January). Helping students develop strategies for effective learning. *Educational Leadership, 46*, 17–19.

CHAPTER 6, TARGETING STAFF DEVELOPMENT

Apple Learning Interchange (2003). Digital learning events. Education event online: Leading in a culture of change resources. Retrieved August 30, 2003, from http://ali.apple.com/ali_sites/ali/exhibits/1000081/Resources.html

Butzin, S., & King, F. J. (1992, Summer). An evaluation of project CHILD. *Florida Technology in Education Quarterly, 4*(4).

Bartunek, H. M. (1990). The classroom teacher as teacher educator. *ERIC Digest*, Washington, D.C.: ERIC Clearinghouse on Teacher Education. Retrieved September 23, 2003, from http://www.ericfacility.net/databases/ERIC_Digests/ed335297.html

Calhoun, E. F. (1994). *How to use action research in the self-renewing school.* Alexandria, VA: Association for Supervision and Curriculum Development.

Center on Reinventing Public Education. (2003). *Making sense of leading schools: A study of the school principalship.* Available from http://www.crpe.org/pubs.shtml

Clune, W. H. (1994, December). The cost and management of program adequacy: An emerging issue in educational policy and finance. *Educational Policy, 8*(4), 365–375.

Committee for Economic Development. (1994). *Putting learning first: Governing and managing the schools for high achievement.* New York: Committee for Economic Development.

Darling-Hammond, L. (1994). *Professional development schools: Schools for developing a profession.* New York: Teachers College Press.

Dilworth, M. E., & Imig, D. G. (1995, Winter). Professional teacher development. *The ERIC Review, 3*(3), 5–11.

ERIC. (1995, June). Reconceptualizing professional teacher development. Retrieved September 19, 2003, from http://www.zuni.k12.nm.us/Ias/21TE/misc/eric2.htm

Feiman-Nemser, S., & Parker, M. (1992, Spring). Mentoring in context: A comparison of two U.S. programs for beginning teachers. NCRTL Special Report, National Center for Research on Teacher Learning, Michigan State University.

Fielding, G. D., & Schalock, H. D. (1985). Promoting the professional development of teachers and administrators. Eugene, OR: ERIC Clearinghouse on Educational Management, Digest Series, 31.

Fullan, M. (2001). *Leading in a culture of change*. San Francisco: Jossey-Bass.

Fullan, M. (2002, January). Interview by Nancy Sellers. Available from http://ali.apple.com

Glidewell, J., et al. (1983). Professional support systems: The teaching profession. In A. Nadler, J. Fisher, & B. Depaulo (eds.), *New directions in helping*. New York: Academic Press.

Goleman, D. (March/April, 2000). Leadership that gets results. *Harvard Business Review*.

Hadderman, M. (2001). Trends and issues: School finance. ERIC Clearinghouse on Educational Management. University of Oregon. Retrieved September 23, 2003, from http://eric.uoregon.edu/trends_issues/finance/

Hall, G. E., & George, A. A. (1979). *Stages of concern about innovation: The concept, initial verification and some implications*. Austin, TX: Research and Development Center for Teacher Education, University of Texas.

Hall, G. E., Wallace, R. C., Jr., & Dossett, W. A. (1973). *A developmental conceptualization of the adoption process within educational institutions*. Austin, TX: Research and Development Center for Teacher Education, University of Texas.

Hanusek, E. A. (1994, December). A jaundiced view of "adequacy" in school finance reform. *Educational Policy*, 8(4), 460–469.

Heifetz, R. (1994). *Leadership without easy answers*. Cambridge, MA: Belknap Press of Harvard University.

Honeyman, D. (1994). Finances and the problems of America's school buildings. *The Clearing House, 68*, 95–97.

Kazal-Thresher, D. M. (1993, March). Educational expenditures and school achievement: When and how money can make a difference. *Educational Researcher,* 30–32.

Kedro, M. J., et al. (2001, May). Eleven selected schools of opportunity: Reform model implementation and achievement. SLPS Division of Research, Assessment and Evaluation.

Kedro, M. J., Short, W. E., et al. (2001, December). Extent of staff professional development in instructional reform models at SLPS schools of opportunity (Spring 2001). SLPS Division of Research, Assessment and Evaluation.

Kedro, M. J. et al. (2002, November). Professional development and MAP test achievement in schools of opportunity. Division of Research, Assessment and Evaluation, St. Louis Public Schools.

Kedro, M. J., & Short, W. E. (in press). What did the teachers know and when did they know it? Evaluating professional development in instructional models [tentative, working title]. *Journal of Staff Development, 25.* National Staff Development Council.

Knowles, M. S. (1970). *The modern practice of adult education: From pedagogy to andragogy.* New York: Association Press.

Kowalski, T. (1995). Chasing the wolves from the schoolhouse door. *Phi Delta Kappan, 76,* 486–489.

Langer, J. (1999). *Excellence in English in middle and high school: How teachers' professional lives support student achievement.* Center for English Learning and Achievement, State University of New York, Albany. Retrieved August 30, 2003, from http://ccla.albany.edu/eie1/main.html

Lays, J. (1991, April). Educating Eddie. *State Legislatures, 17*(4), 20–22.

Levin, H. M. (1989, Spring). Financing the education of at-risk students. *Educational Evaluation and Policy Analysis, 11*(1), 47–60.

Little, J. (1982). Norms of collegiality and experimentation: Workplace conditions and school success. *American Educational Research Journal, 19*(3), 325–340.

Little, J. (1993). Teacher's professional development in a climate of education reform. *Educational Evaluation and Policy Analysis, 15*(2), 129–151.

McLean, J. E. (1995). *Improving education through action research: A guide for administrators and teachers.* Thousand Oaks, CA: Corwin Press.

Miles, K. H., & Darling-Hammond, L. (1998, Spring). Rethinking the allocation of teaching resources: Some lessons from high-performing schools. *Educational Evaluation and Policy Analysis, 20*(1), 9–29.

National Center for Education Statistics. (1999). How old are America's public schools? *Issue Brief.* U.S. Dept. of Education, Office of Educational Research and Improvement.

Natriello, G. (1981). Teacher's perceptions of the frequency of evaluation and assessments of their effort and effectiveness. *American Educational Research Journal, 21*(3), 1–4.

North Central Regional Educational Laboratory. (1996). Critical issues: Realizing new learning for all students through professional development. Retrieved

September 19, 2003, from http://www.ncrel.org/sdrs/areas/issues/educatrs/ profdevl/pd200.htm

Odden, A. (1994, May). Including school finance in systemic reform strategies: A commentary. *CPRE Finance Brief.* New Brunswick, NJ: Consortium for Policy Research in Education.

Odden, A., & Busch, C. (1998). *Financing schools for high performance: Strategies for improving the use of educational resources.* San Francisco: Jossey-Bass.

Oswald, L. J. (1995, August). Priority on learning: Efficient use of resources. ERIC Digest 100. Clearinghouse on Educational Management, University of Oregon. Retreived September 19, 2003, from http://www.eric.uoregon.edu/ publications/digests/digest100.html

Parsad, B., Lewis, L., & Farris, E. (2001, Fall). Teacher preparation and professional development: 2000. *Education Statistics Quarterly, 3,* 33–36.

Smylie, M., & Conyers, J. (1991, Winter). Changing conceptions of teaching influence the future of staff development. *Journal of Staff Development, 12*(1), 12–16.

Sparks, D. (2000, March). Corporate lessons for evaluating staff development. *Results.* National Staff Development Council. Retrieved August 30, 2003, from http://www.nsdc.org/library/results/res3-00spar.html

Svede, V., Jeudy-Hugo, D., & Begley, P. (1996). School leadership: A profile document. Retrieved August 30, 2003, from http://www.oise.utoronto. ca/~vsvede/

Tasmania Department of Education, Community, and Cultural Development (Australia). (1997). Does information technology improve student learning outcomes? A concise summary overview of Ryan (1991), Kulik & Kulik (1991), Fitzgerald et al. (1996), Robinson (1994), Harris (1994), and more than 30 other sources on technology applications.

Tye, K. A. & Tye, B. (1984). Teacher isolation and school reform. *Phi Delta Kappan, 65*(5), 319–322.

U.S. Dept. of Education. (1987). Collegiality and teacher supervision. In *What works: Research about teaching and learning* (2nd ed.).

U.S. Dept. of Education [Westat & Policy Studies Associates]. (2001). *The longitudinal evaluation of school change and performance (LESCP) in Title 1 schools.* Available at http://www.ed.gov/offices/OUS/PES/esed/ lescp_highlights.html

Wallace, R. C., Jr. (1996). *From vision to practice: The art of educational leadership.* Thousand Oaks, CA: Corwin Press.

Zimpher, N., & Ashburn, E. (1992). Countering parochialism in teacher candidates. In M. Dilworth (ed.), *Diversity in teacher education: New expectations*. San Francisco: Jossey-Bass.

CHAPTER 7, OVERCOMING RESISTANCE AND UNLOCKING POTENTIAL

Association of Washington School Principals. (1998–2003). Professional reading list: Instructional leadership, data driven decision making, and community leadership. Retrieved October 26, 2003, from http://www.awsp.org/Foundation/LeadershipGrant/pfsl-bookshelf.htm

Aubrey, J. V. (1992, July). The principal's leadership role in effective site-based managed elementary schools. University of Bridgeport (Connecticut) doctoral dissertation. Summary may be retrieved from http://www.media.wiley.com/assets/49/45/bus_lc_jb_aubrey.pdf

Buckingham, M., & Clifton, D. O. (2001). *Now, discover your strengths*. New York: Free Press and Gallup Organization. Information and excerpts may be retrieved from http://www.gallup.com/publications/strengths.asp, http://www.strengthsfinder.com, and http://www.education.gallup.com/content/default.asp?ci=892

Carrison, D., & Walsh, R. (1998). *Semper fi: Business leadership the Marine Corps way*. New York: Amacom Books.

Gallup Education Division. (2003). Principal leadership series. Retrieved October 26, 2003, from http://www.education.gallup.com/content/default.asp?ci=859

Grimmett, P. P., Rostad, O. P., & Ford, B. (1992). The transformation of supervision. In C. D. Glickman (ed.), *Supervision in transition: 1992 yearbook of the Association for Supervision and Curriculum Development*. Alexandria, VA: Association for Supervision and Curriculum Development.

International Center for Leadership in Education. (n.d.). Mega analysis: The challenges facing schools. Retrieved October 26, 2003, from http://www.daleicle.org/megaanalysis.pdf

Interstate School Leaders Licensure Consortium. (n.d.). Standards for school leaders. Council of Chief State School Officers. Retrieved October 26, 2003, from http://www.awsp.org/LeaderDev/Intern?intern-isllc-stand.htm

Knapp, M. S., Copland, M. A., & Talbert, J. E. (2003, February). Leading for learning: Reflective tools for school and district leaders. Center for the Study of Teaching and Policy, University of Washington. U.S. OERI and Wallace–Reader's Digest Funds. Retrieved October 4, 2003, from http://www.ctpweb.org

Marzano, R. (2003). *What works in schools: Translating research into action.* Alexandria, VA: Association for Supervision and Curriculum Development. Information and excerpts may be retrieved from http://www.ascd.org/publications/books/102271/chapter2.html

MeansBusiness. (2000). Concept book summary: A unique concept database of 20,000 key ideas from business and management books. Retrieved October 23, 2003, from http://www.meansbusiness.com/learnlandc.asp, http://www.meansbusiness.com/Leadership-and-Change-Books/, and http://www.leadershipandchangebooks.com/

Mohr, N., & Dichter, A. (2003, January). Stages of team development: Lessons from the struggles of site-based management. Annenberg Institute for School Reform at Brown University. Retrieved November 5, 2003, from http://www.annenberginstitute.org/publications/stages.html

Perry, G. S., Jr., & McDermott, J. (2003, August). Learning and leading: Rethinking district-school relationships. New Horizons for Learning, Seattle, WA. Retrieved October 7, 2003, from http://www.newhorizons.org/trans/perry.htm

Quinn, R. E. (1996). *Deep change: Discovering the leader within.* San Francisco: Jossey-Bass.

Spreitzer, G., & Quinn, R. E. (1996, September). Empowering middle managers to be transformational leaders. *Journal of Applied Behavioral Science.*

Tracy, B. (2003). Capitalizing on your strengths. Retrieved October 12, 2003, from http://www.successreview.com/BTarticle02.htm

CHAPTER 8, PUTTING IT ALL TOGETHER

American Association of School Librarians. (2001, April 18). Role of the school library media specialist in site-based management. Retrieved November 11, 2003, from http://archive.ala.org/aasl/positions/ps_sitemgmt.html

American Association of School Librarians. (2003). Resource guides for school library media program development. Retrieved November 11, 2003, from http://www.ala.org/aaslTemplate.cfm?Section=Resource_Guides& Template=/ContentManagement/ContentDisplay.cfm&ContentID=14760

Index

About the Author

M. James Kedro is a senior evaluator for the St. Louis public schools and an adjunct professor of history at St. Louis Community College–Meramec. Dr. Kedro received his Ph.D. from the University of Denver and is listed in *Who's Who in the World*. He has authored articles in a variety of journals and currently resides in Grantwood Village, Missouri.